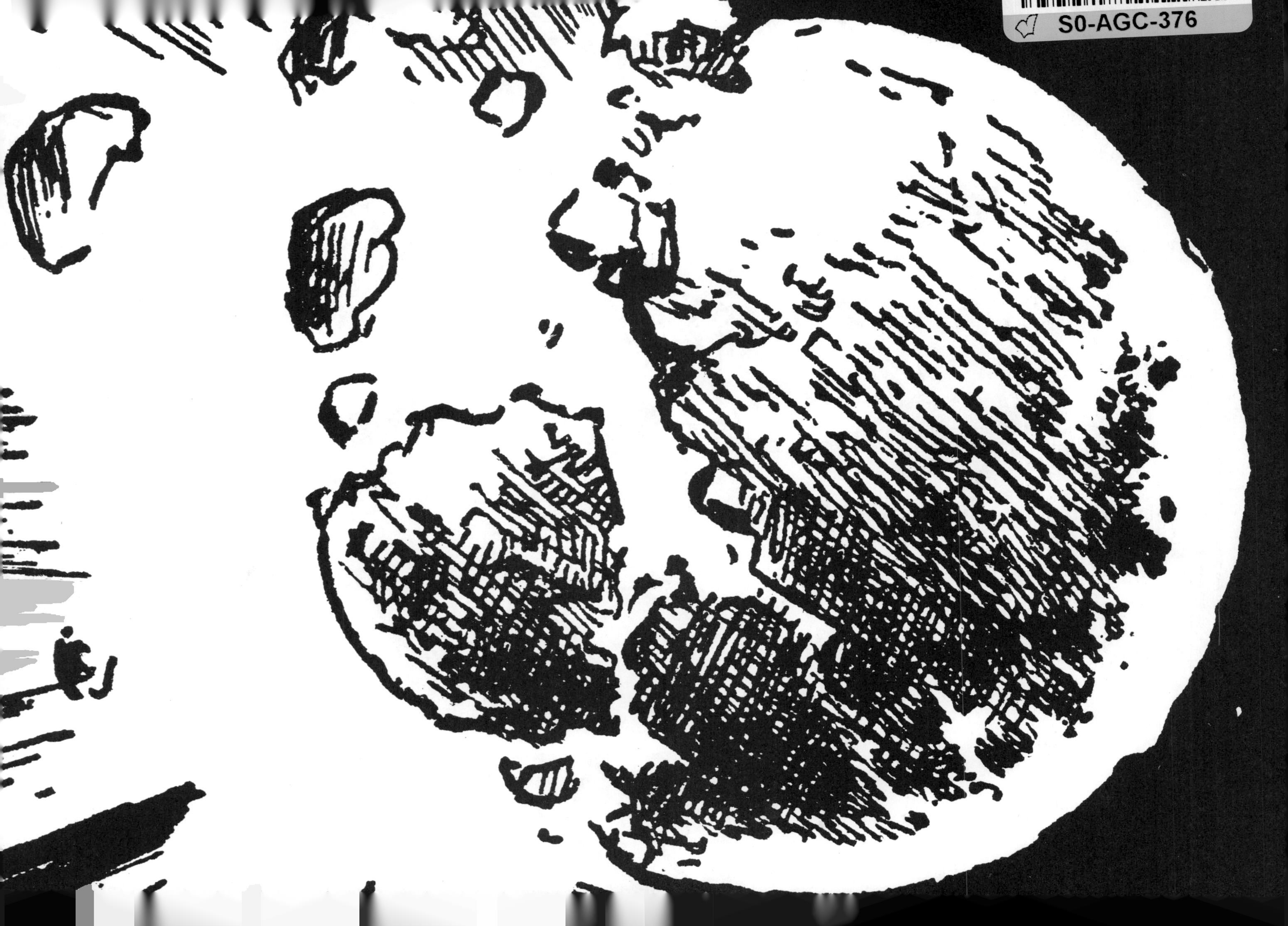

SUPERMAN®
THE DAILIES

VOLUME I: Strips 1-306, 1939-1940

Created by
Jerry Siegel and Joe Shuster

DC COMICS
New York, New York

KITCHEN SINK PRESS
Northampton, Massachusetts

This book would not have been possible without these professionals who were, in one way or another, originally involved with the Superman comic strip:
Jerry Siegel, Joe Shuster, Paul Cassidy, Wayne Boring, John Sikela, Jack Schiff, Whitney Ellsworth, and Harry Donenfeld and Vincent Sullivan.

The editors would like to thank the following individuals for lending rare source material, without which this collection would not have been possible:
Mitch Itkowitz, Bill Blackbeard (Director) and the San Francisco Academy of Comic Art, Rick Norwood, Jeffrey Lindenblatt.

Library of Congress Cataloging-in-Publication Data

Siegel, Jerry, 1914–
Superman : the dailies / created by Jerry Siegel and Joe Shuster.
p. cm.
Contents: v. 1. Featuring strips 1 thru 306, January 16, 1939 to Jan. 6, 1940 — v. 2. Featuring strips 307 thru 678: Jan. 8, 1940 to Mar. 8, 1941 — v. 3. Featuring strips 673 thru 966 : Mar. 10, 1941 to Feb. 14, 1942.
ISBN 1-56389-460-2 (v. 1). — ISBN 1-56389-461-0 (v. 2.). — ISBN 1-56389-462-9 (v. 3)
I. Shuster, Joe. II. Title.
PN6728.S9S5477 1999 98-27875
741.5'973—dc21 CIP

First Printing: 1999 **Printed in Canada.** **Visit the KSP and DC Comics Web sites at www.kitchensink.com & www.dccomics.com!**

SUPERMAN: The Dailies, Volume 1, 1939–1940. Copublished by DC Comics, 1700 Broadway, New York, NY 10019, and Kitchen Sink Press, 76 Pleasant Street, Northampton, MA 01060.

CONTENTS
VOLUME I

A JOB FOR SUPERMAN

James Vance

Jerry Siegel (top) & Joe Shuster

When Paul Cassidy answered a "help wanted" advertisement in 1938, all he wanted was a way to make a few extra bucks. Money was scarce in that Depression year, and the prospect of a steady supplement to his art instructor's income was worth the gamble of a trip from Milwaukee to Cleveland.

His prospective employers turned out to be a pair of young men in their early twenties. They were running a no-frills operation—the interview took place in an apartment where one of the young men lived with his parents—but their money was real enough, and the supply of work was steady. His trip a success, Cassidy returned home with those few extra bucks secure . . . little realizing that he had just gotten in on the ground floor of comics history.

The job was "ghosting" artwork for "Slam Bradley," "Spy," "Federal Men" and "Radio Squad," serialized stories created for the infant comic book field. His new employers were Jerry Siegel and Joe Shuster, an ambitious writer-artist team who had been contributing features to such titles as *More Fun, Detective,* and *Adventure Comics* for three years. By 1938, it had become clear that Shuster needed some help in the art department, and so they took out the ad which brought Paul Cassidy to the Shuster family home.

As it turned out, the ambitious young Clevelanders were going to need all the help they could get, for another of their creations had just debuted in the first issue of *Action Comics* (cover-dated June 1938, the same month as Cassidy's interview). Siegel and Shuster were optimistic about the new feature, but they had no idea just how busy they were about to become. No one could have predicted the colossal success of Superman.

Only a year later, when the strips reprinted in this volume first appeared in daily newspapers, the Man of Steel had already captured the public's imagination. Simply by virtue of appearing in comic books (and spawning a succession of imitators that continues to the present day), Superman had put that struggling industry on the map. Within another two years, he would be a star of radio and silver screen, and a merchandising bonanza—but more than any other incarnation, it was as a newspaper strip that Superman fulfilled his creators' dreams of success.

The appeal may be lost on younger readers these days, but there was a time when newspaper syndication was the Big Time for adventure cartoonists. Until Superman came along, imaginative action heroes like Flash Gordon, The Phantom, and Buck Rogers had few peers outside of the daily paper. It was the logical place to find a Man of Steel.

It was also a respectable place. "The media" have taken their lumps in recent years, treated with contempt by high-placed scoundrels trying to cover their own moral lapses by tarnishing the images of the agencies that report them—but in 1939, the press was respected by the public and feared by the corrupt. Decades before Woodward and Bernstein brought the notion back into vogue with their exposure of the Watergate scandal, journalists were seen as heroes who battled social injustice—a conviction and a concern obviously shared by Siegel and Shuster.

Their enthusiasm was clear and nearly palpable: not only was the early Superman the ultimate social reformer, he was also a reporter. In a day when radio, movies, and the printed page were virtually overrun by fearless fictional journalists, the nation's children knew that the most heroic reporters of them all were Clark Kent and Lois Lane.

To be sure, it was Kent's exploits as the last Son of Krypton that gave the stories their high-voltage excitement—but even when the Man of Steel wasn't around, it seemed that Clark and Lois were forever being threatened, kidnapped, and nearly murdered by gangsters and lowlifes in high places . . . *just because they were reporters.* What red-blooded American kid could resist a lifestyle like that?

It was an enthusiasm that the youthful creators of Superman shared with their readers. Long before the famous costume was designed, even before the Kryptonian origin was conceived, one fact was already firm in the mind of writer Jerry Siegel: Superman would also be known as Clark Kent, reporter. In the years leading up to the feature's debut in *Action Comics,* Siegel and Shuster occasionally flirted with the notion of submitting their creation to the fledgling comic book industry—but both were firmly convinced that the proper home for Superman was in the pages of the nation's newspapers.

CLARK KENT
SUPERMAN
ONE AND SAME!

Friends since their high school days, Siegel and Shuster had spent the Depression decade trying to sell comic strip ideas to newspaper syndicates. Typical apprentice work, "Reggie Van Twerp," "Goober, The Mighty," "Interplanetary Police," and other concepts were either overly ambitious or too reflective of their inspirations, and were rejected.

However, despite its roots in such science fiction novels as Philip Wylie's *Gladiator* and, later, John W. Campbell's *The Mightiest Machine, Superman* was an original; and though it seemed that he couldn't sell it to save his life, Siegel never lost faith in the power of the concept.

It isn't generally known that before embarking on their legendary string of rejections, Siegel and Shuster actually put together a comic book version of *Superman* in 1933. That was the year they saw the debut of the magazines traditionally called the first true comic books: *Funnies on Parade, Famous Funnies,* and *Century of Comics,* pioneer publications that offered reprinted adventures of Joe Palooka, Mutt and Jeff, and other newspaper characters.

And then there was *Detective Dan,* which managed to be a true curiosity in a field that had only just come into being. *Detective Dan* measured 9 1/2 by 12 inches while the competition was a handier 7 1/2 by 10 inches, and offered thirty-six black and white pages, as opposed to the brightly colored interiors of *Famous Funnies* and company. What made it a true anomaly in the field, though, was the fact that its contents had never been seen before. *Detective Dan*, featuring the adventures of a plainclothesman who bore a suspicious resemblance to Dick Tracy, was the first comic book to offer original material.

Siegel and Shuster sold *Detective Dan*'s publisher, Humor Publishing Company, on the idea of bringing out a comic book devoted to their fantastic brainchild. Titled *The Superman* and featuring the exploits of a physical marvel who performed his amazing feats clad in slacks and a T-shirt, the entire comic book was drawn and submitted—but at the last minute, Humor Publishing backed out of the arrangement. *Detective Dan* hadn't sold well, and the publisher was too smart to lose more money by printing anything as commercially dubious as a comic book about a superhero.

It's possible that this 1933 *Superman* might have made the same kind of history as the version that finally saw the light of day in 1938; it's more likely, however, that neither the tiny comic book market nor the talents of Siegel and Shuster were sufficiently developed for the same kind of lightning to have struck five years earlier. Had the 1933 version seen print, it might have become nothing more than a small footnote in the history of publishing, and the comic book field might have developed in an entirely different direction than it has since the appearance of *Action Comics* no. 1.

A SCIENCE FICTION STORY in CARTOONS
The SUPERMAN
THE MOST ASTOUNDING FICTION CHARACTER OF ALL TIME
10¢

At this point, it's impossible to do more than speculate on the subject, for upon receiving the rejection, a despondent Shuster tore up his original art and threw it into the fireplace. Today only the cover for that aborted version of *Superman* remains, rescued by Siegel at the last moment from fiery oblivion.

With no future for Superman in comic books, Siegel turned his ambitions again to the syndicated strip. He approached several artists as possible collaborators, but ultimately returned to Shuster. They turned out several weeks of continuity, and began the long and heartbreaking process of getting rejected by every syndicate in the business. It must have been particularly galling to receive letters advising them, as Bell Syndicate's did, that *Superman* lacked "extraordinary appeal" or, as United Features summarized, that it was "a rather immature piece of work"—especially when the clumsily written and crudely drawn knockoff *Detective Dan* was now appearing in daily newspapers under the title *Dan Dunn*.

If the young collaborators were bitter, though, it didn't slow them down. While continuing to wallpaper their bedrooms with rejections slips, they began developing other features, and some of them actually sold.

It was comic books where they finally broke into print with the pulpy supernatural adventures of "Dr. Occult," which began appearing in *New Fun* (later *More Fun) Comics* no. 6, dated October 1935. That one-page strip (it would soon double in length) debuted in the same issue as another Siegel & Shuster production, the swashbuckling "Henri Duval"—which ran for only a few installments before its creators abandoned it for the more commercial uniformed cop saga "Radio Squad."

On a roll at last, the boys created "Federal Men" for the second issue of *New* (later *New Adventure*, and finally simply *Adventure) Comics*.

Superman hadn't been forgotten in this busy time, but a look at Siegel and Shuster's 1935–38 output indicates that they were beginning to cannibalize him for parts. The

IN HIS LABORATORY, DR OCCULT BINDS THE IMPRISONED WERE-WOLF WITH CHAINS, THEN SEATS HIMSELF AND PATIENTLY WAITS FOR DAWN ——
Doctor Occult

adventures of brawling private eye Slam Bradley borrowed the dynamic approach the team had planned for the Man of Steel, resulting in eye-popping action sequences that opened up the comic book page as never before. Dr. Occult not only had Superman's face, he had become a superhero himself in a 1936 storyline, receiving magical powers and trading in his tuxedo and trench coat for a pair of tights and a cape. Even the adventures of Steve Carson in "Federal Men" began to reflect the fantastic milieu in which Superman would have operated; in addition to more prosaic menaces, the G-Man had to contend with a giant robot, and encountered a character named Jor-L.

Before the entire concept could be ground up like sausage, however, there was a lucky break. *Superman* had been submitted several times to the McClure Syndicate, only to be returned on each occasion. While in the syndicate offices, it came to the attention of young cartoonist Sheldon Mayer, who was assisting M. C. Gaines in the production of comic books which were printed for various publishers on presses owned by McClure. After several tries, Mayer convinced Gaines that the outlandish feature had merit.

Gaines could have tried to influence the syndicate to give the strip a try, but he was a businessman, not a philanthropist—so he pitched the project to one of his clients. Stories differ about whether the publisher Harry Donenfeld or editor Vincent Sullivan made the decision, but the bottom line is that *Superman* was sold at last . . . to the company that had been publishing Siegel and Shuster all along.

Siegel and Shuster chopped up their syndicate submission, cropping some panels, expanding others, and pasting the whole thing up into a thirteen-page story. Gaines got the printing business, and Detective Comics, Inc. (now DC Comics) was the owner of a gold mine that would spin off into other comic books and every kind of merchandise imaginable—including a newspaper strip issued by the McClure Syndicate.

Superman first appeared in the newspapers on January 16, 1939. The *Houston Chronicle* was the first subscriber, followed immediately by the *Milwaukee Journal* and the *San Antonio Express*. By the end of the year, sixty papers were carrying the feature, and there were more to come.

Back in Milwaukee, Paul Cassidy found his evenings and weekends devoted more and more to the adventures of Superman. In addition to comic book pages featuring Slam, "Spy," and the gang, he produced 149 daily installments of the *Superman* strip before his bosses asked him to move to Cleveland and work full-time. They offered him sixty-four dollars a week, an offer you couldn't refuse in 1939.

He was joined there by Wayne Boring, a young man who'd been turning out advertising art for the Norfolk *Virginia Pilot*. Boring had answered the 1938 ad, too, and had arrived in Cleveland a couple of weeks before Cassidy. Eventually, they would be joined by Leo Novak and John Sikela in the tiny office space that housed the Siegel and Shuster shop.

The shop, according to Cassidy, was "a small setup. We had a reception room and a main office; Joe worked in there, and Wayne Boring and myself.

"Wayne was a very pleasant fellow," Cassidy recalled in a 1994 interview, "and Siegel and Shuster were polite and good company, but everybody was too busy to do much chatting or socializing.

"Joe was in every day, but he wasn't a talkative fellow. He'd spend most of his time inking in the faces and eating candy bars. So Wayne and I came in every day, got our scripts, kept our noses to the drawing board and turned in our jobs. I was doing thirteen pages a week and some of the dailies, so we couldn't have had much time off if we'd wanted it.

"I did all kinds of stuff, from pencilling to lettering to inking everything but the faces. Shuster's vision was pretty bad then, but he still inked all the faces."

Character faces, in fact, were just about the only aspect of the artwork created in the studio that Shuster kept under tight personal control. In some shops, the assistants were forced to slavishly imitate a house style, but Shuster and Siegel gave their artists much more autonomy. The result, as a perusal of this volume will reveal, was that the strips signed by Shuster were a stylistic hodgepodge—but it indicates that Siegel and Shuster hadn't let their hard-won success swell their heads.

"They were very easy to work with," said Cassidy. "They didn't interfere in any way with how we interpreted the script. It was just at the beginning then, and I'm not sure they realized in the early days what they had going on for them, that *Superman* was going to become as big a deal as it did."

Siegel, of course, didn't have a bullpen of writers, and he was still scripting all of the older features in addition to the *Superman* dailies and comic books. Wayne Boring recalled that the publishers tried to persuade Siegel to drop everything else and concentrate on *Superman*, but Siegel refused; not only did he want to continue taking advantage of the great opportunities that he had been given in the post-Depression era, they were *all* his characters, and he wanted to keep on controlling their destinies.

But Siegel was no prima donna. "Jerry did most of his writing at home," said Cassidy, "and would come in every once in a while with his scripts. The scripts would indicate what the action was and, of course, what the conversation was, but there was not too much guidance. The picturization of the script was basically up to Wayne and me. We were never asked to do anything over or change it."

With six installments a week of daily strip continuity to fill, plus well over fifty pages of comic books a month, Siegel may have wondered what he'd gotten himself into; certainly, a few of these early newspaper adventures seem to be less the product of inspiration than the need to meet deadlines.

The earliest sequences bore a marked resemblance to material that had already appeared in comic books. Here and there panels can be spotted that are redrawn versions of some used in *Action Comics*, and the earliest storylines are clearly reworkings of previously published material.

The daily strip was more than just a hack job, though. Its serial format and more leisurely pacing allowed Siegel to tell stories for which the comic book was unsuitable—and when the young writer was on a roll, he turned out continuities that were not only exciting, but heartfelt. At times, they even contributed elements to the property's basic framework that endure to this day.

The most notable example is the strip's opening sequence, a two-week continuity which marked the first detailed account of the famous origin story. *Action Comics* no. 1 had disposed of the subject in a single panel that read, "As a distant planet was destroyed by old age, a scientist placed his infant son within a hastily devised space-ship, launching it toward Earth!" Not until the daily strip appeared did its readers learn that the scientist was named Jor-L, that our hero was born of an amazing race of supermen, and that the "distant planet" was called Krypton.

When these strips first saw print, many of the details were still being worked out. For instance, the familiar figure of *Daily Planet* editor Perry White would not appear in the comic books until late 1940, and even later than that in the daily strips. In the beginning, Clark Kent and Lois Lane reported to George Taylor of the *Daily Star* (and once, in the second issue of *Action Comics*, the *Cleveland Evening News*). Without explanation, Taylor became the editor of the *Daily Planet* in the November 20, 1939 strip (and in the April 1940 issue of *Action Comics*). It was a minimal difference, really, but also a clear indicator to latter-day readers that even as he was beginning to take the nation by storm, the Superman we know today was still in the process of being born.

As noted, the Superman of the comic books wasn't shy about tackling social problems, nor was he subtle: at times it seemed that wife-beaters, slumlords, and war profiteers who felt his wrath were lucky to escape with their lives—and some didn't. Siegel would soon begin exploring the same themes with greater sophistication—largely because DC editor Whitney Ellsworth would impose a moral code that forbade Superman from using his powers to kill anyone, even a villain. The strips reprinted in this volume, however, reflect the earlier approach: a distinctive combination of escapist fantasy that was particularly appealing to young readers, plus vigilante social reform for their parents—America's working men and women.

Fighting graft and corruption, ending wars and reviving faded careers, rescuing orphans and princesses—all the while crashing through walls, defying bombs and bullets, and outracing natural disasters . . . *that's* the essential Superman of Siegel and Shuster, the original genuine article whose adventures fill this volume.

SUPERMAN
comes to
MORTISE AND INSERT
NAME OF CITY
WHAM!
SUPERMAN'S steely muscles make it child's play for him to toss an automobile with his hands!
SUPERMAN'S physical make-up enables him to leap great distances and vault sky-scrapers!
SUPERMAN is a perfect creature from another planet — he amazes this world with spectacular feats of daring and strength. His courage is greater than that of the mightiest warrior — his skill surpasses all others in every astonishing feat that he attempts. Young and old will be delighted with the amazing triumphs of SUPERMAN!
Posing as CLARK KENT SUPERMAN tracks down crime!
Disguised as Clark Kent, reporter, he foresees disasters—and in his own daring character of SUPER-MAN he solves crimes, saves lives, helps whole communities!
BUT--BUT WHY THE UNEXPECTED VISIT?
YOU DON'T KNOW IT YET, CLARK, BUT I'M GOING TO THAT ROYAL RECEPTION WITH YOU!
LOIS LANE, of the Lovelorn Column, despises CLARK KENT but adores SUPER-MAN, not knowing they are one and the same!
READ HIS ADVENTURES DAILY ON THE COMIC PAGE—WEEKLY IN FULL COLOR, TOO!
NAME OF PAPER
newest-Most EXCITING Adventure strip

Paul Cassidy, whose work appears throughout these early sequences, remained with the shop until August 1940, when he returned to Milwaukee about the same time his colleagues were packing up and relocating the shop to New York; he continued to work through the mail until early 1942. He resumed his teaching job until 1944, when he joined the *World Book Encyclopedia* staff, eventually becoming its art director.

With the exception of a six-week continuity which he wrote for the *Red Ryder* daily strip and a one-shot comic book feature called "Hemisphere Patrol," the years with Siegel and Shuster constituted his entire comics career, a total output of 173 daily *Superman* strips and eight Sunday pages, plus 630 comics pages and seven covers—by his estimate, "about 8800 pictures or panels" in all.

"I could see that comics was not really a future for me," said Cassidy, "so I came back to Milwaukee. I haven't regretted it."

Nor did he regret the time he'd spent with Siegel and Shuster; after all, he'd met some interesting people and contributed to the creation of one of the most enduring popular characters of the twentieth centruy.

And he'd made those few extra bucks that he'd needed so badly in the first place. Having been given a helping hand by the Man of Steel himself, Paul Cassidy knew the true value of a job for Superman.

EPISODE ONE
SUPERMAN COMES TO EARTH

Superman—By Jerry Siegel and Joe Shuster *The Superman Is Born* (Copyright, 1939.)

KRYPTON, A DISTANT PLANET SO FAR ADVANCED IN EVOLUTION THAT IT BEARS A CIVILIZATION OF SUPERMEN -- BEINGS WHICH REPRESENT THE HUMAN RACE AT ITS ULTIMATE PEAK OF PERFECT DEVELOPMENT!
MILE AFTER MILE STREAKS BY AS JOR-L, KRYPTON'S FOREMOST SCIENTIST, RACES ALONG AT A TERRIFIC SPEED THAT WOULD OUT-DISTANCE THE FASTEST EXPRESS TRAIN...
... A GREAT LEAP CARRIES JOR-L HUNDREDS OF YARDS INTO THE AIR TO A BALCONY NEAR THE TOP OF HIS HOME
JOR-L! YOU'VE COME!
AS QUICKLY AS I COULD! LORA, MY BELOVED! WHERE IS HE -- OUR NEWBORN SON?

uperman—By Jerry Siegel and Joe Shuster *Destruction Menaces* (Copyright, 1939.)

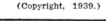

JOR-L, I'M AFRAID OUR NEWBORN SON, KAL-L, IS RATHER A ROUGHNECK! HE GAVE THE DOCTOR A DISCOLORED EYE, AND I'VE HAD DIFFICULTY IN PREVENTING HIS LEAPING FROM MY ARMS!
JUST LIKE YOUR DAD!
ARE YOU HAPPY, DEAR?
MORE THAN I CAN EVER--
SUDDENLY, THE ROOM BEGINS TO QUIVER! FIRST SLOWLY.... THEN WITH INCREASING VIOLENCE...
JOR-L! W-WHAT--?
AN EARTH-QUAKE!
CLUTCHED IN THE TREMORS' MERCILESS FURY, JOR-L'S HOME COMMENCES TO TOPPLE BEFORE THE TERRIFIC STRAIN!

Superman—By Jerry Siegel and Joe Shuster *Safe!* (Copyright, 1939.)

CRASH
LORA . . . KAL-L . . . UNDER THAT WRECKAGE! I'VE GOT TO SAVE THEM!
LORA! YOU'RE ALL RIGHT -- BOTH OF YOU?
YES. -- BUT THERE HAVE BEEN SO MANY TERRIBLE EARTHQUAKES RECENTLY? -- WHY?

Superman—By Jerry Siegel and Joe Shuster *The Terrible Truth!* (Copyright, 1939.)

ON THE WAY TO JOR-L'S OTHER RESIDENCE . .
BUT YOU HAVEN'T ANSWERED ME. -- WHY ARE WE EXPERIENCING SO MANY EARTHQUAKES, LATELY?
THAT'S EXACTLY WHAT I INTEND TO FIND OUT!
UPON REACHING THEIR DESTINATION, JOR-L HURRIES INTO HIS LABORATORY AND BECOMES IMMERSED IN HIS CALCULATIONS
HOURS PASS . . . THEN DAYS . . .
PLEASE TAKE THIS FOOD!
I TOLD YOU I WAS, NOT TO BE DISTURBED!
AND THEN, ON THE FIFTH DAY, JOR-L LEARNS THE TERRIBLE TRUTH . . .
NO! I MUST BE WRONG -- I MUST!

Superman—By Jerry Siegel and Joe Shuster

Krypton Doomed!

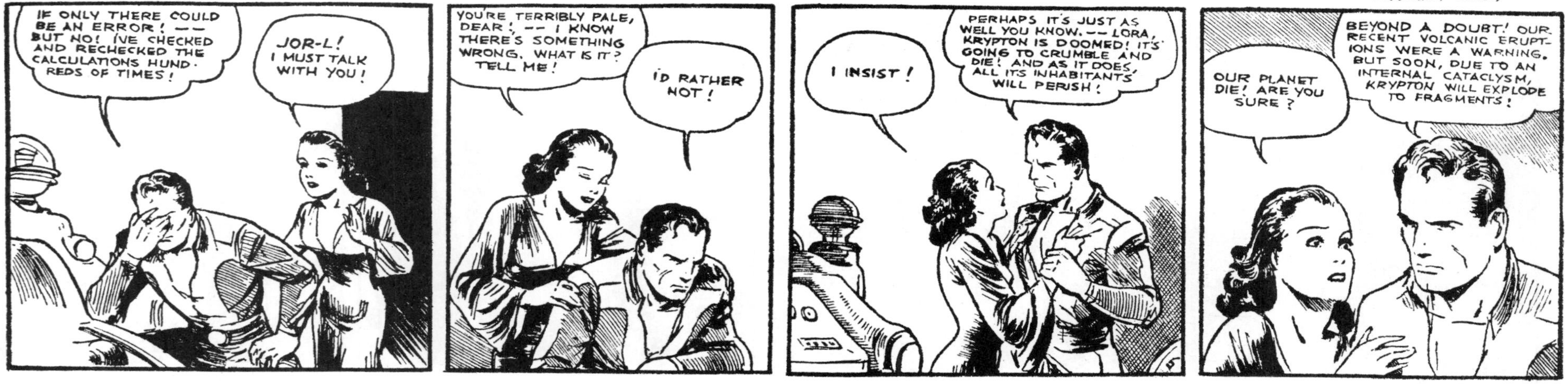
IF ONLY THERE COULD BE AN ERROR! -- BUT NO! I'VE CHECKED AND RECHECKED THE CALCULATIONS HUNDREDS OF TIMES!
JOR-L! I MUST TALK WITH YOU!
YOU'RE TERRIBLY PALE, DEAR! -- I KNOW THERE'S SOMETHING WRONG. WHAT IS IT? TELL ME!
I'D RATHER NOT!
I INSIST!
PERHAPS IT'S JUST AS WELL YOU KNOW. -- LORA, KRYPTON IS DOOMED! IT'S GOING TO CRUMBLE AND DIE! AND AS IT DOES, ALL ITS INHABITANTS WILL PERISH!
OUR PLANET DIE! ARE YOU SURE?
BEYOND A DOUBT! OUR RECENT VOLCANIC ERUPTIONS WERE A WARNING. BUT SOON, DUE TO AN INTERNAL CATACLYSM, KRYPTON WILL EXPLODE TO FRAGMENTS!

Superman—By Jerry Siegel and Joe Shuster

A Solution

HOW PEACEFULLY OUR LITTLE DARLING SLEEPS! HE'S TOO LOST IN SLUMBER TO BE BOTHERED BY THE FACT THAT SOON OUR WORLD WILL BE TORN ASUNDER, KILLING US ALL!
LORA, IT'S NOT RIGHT FOR HIM TO DIE! HE'S YOUNG.. HE'S ENTITLED TO A RICH, FULL LIFE.. AND WE'D MADE SUCH WONDERFUL PLANS FOR HIM!
HOW FREE AND ALOOF THOSE STARS ARE! HOW DISTANT FROM THE IMPENDING DOOM! OH, JOR-L! IF ONLY WE, TOO, COULD BE UP THERE, SAFE TO PURSUE OUR LIVES AS WE PLEASE!
LORA!..LORA, YOU'VE STRUCK UPON THE SOLUTION!
I'VE WHAT?
UP THERE! AMONG THOSE STARS! THERE LIES OUR SECURITY! -- I'LL BUILD A SHIP... AN ARK OF SPACE! WE'LL TRANSPORT OUR PLANET'S ENTIRE POPULACE TO ANOTHER WORLD! ...THEN, BY ALL THE POWERS, LET KRYPTON GLOW ITSELF TO ETERNITY -- FOR ALL WE CARE!

Superman—By Jerry Siegel and Joe Shuster

No One Believes Him

(Copyright, 1939.)

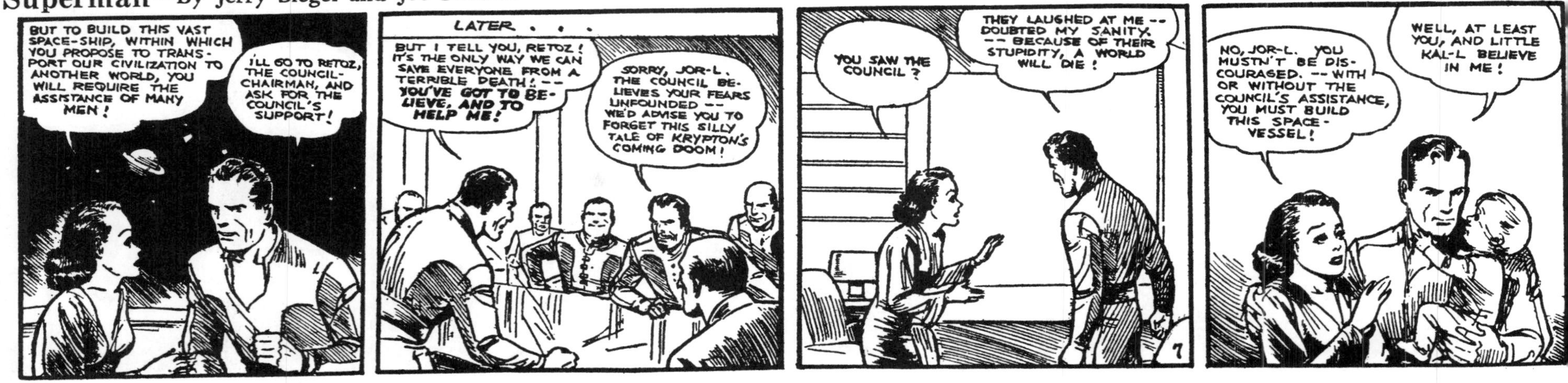
BUT TO BUILD THIS VAST SPACE-SHIP, WITHIN WHICH YOU PROPOSE TO TRANSPORT OUR CIVILIZATION TO ANOTHER WORLD, YOU WILL REQUIRE THE ASSISTANCE OF MANY MEN!
I'LL GO TO RETOZ, THE COUNCIL-CHAIRMAN, AND ASK FOR THE COUNCIL'S SUPPORT!
LATER . . .
BUT I TELL YOU, RETOZ! IT'S THE ONLY WAY WE CAN SAVE EVERYONE FROM A TERRIBLE DEATH! -- YOU'VE GOT TO BELIEVE, AND TO HELP ME!
SORRY, JOR-L. THE COUNCIL BELIEVES YOUR FEARS UNFOUNDED -- WE'D ADVISE YOU TO FORGET THIS SILLY TALE OF KRYPTON'S COMING DOOM!
YOU SAW THE COUNCIL?
THEY LAUGHED AT ME -- DOUBTED MY SANITY. -- BECAUSE OF THEIR STUPIDITY, A WORLD WILL DIE!
NO, JOR-L. YOU MUSTN'T BE DISCOURAGED. -- WITH OR WITHOUT THE COUNCIL'S ASSISTANCE, YOU MUST BUILD THIS SPACE-VESSEL!
WELL, AT LEAST YOU, AND LITTLE KAL-L BELIEVE IN ME!

Superman—By Jerry Siegel and Joe Shuster

A Strange Ship

(Copyright, 1939.)

MONTH FOLLOWS MONTH IN FEVERISH ACTIVITY AS JOR-L PITS HIS MIGHTY BRAIN AGAINST THE NUMEROUS OBSTACLES TO INTERPLANETARY TRAVEL. THEN --
I'VE FINISHED IT, LORA! THE MODEL SPACE-FLIER . . . IT'S READY FOR THE TRIAL JOURNEY!
THAT'S GRAND!
AS YOU SEE, IT'S REALLY NOTHING BUT A MERE TOY. BUT SHOULD ITS AUTOMATICALLY GUIDED FLIGHT TO EARTH PROVE SUCCESSFUL, I'LL COMMENCE TO CONSTRUCT A GIANT SPACE SHIP AT ONCE!
THE PLANET EARTH?
YES. TELESCOPIC OBSERVATION HAS CONVINCED ME THAT EARTH IS THE ONLY NEARBY PLANET CAPABLE OF SUPPORTING LIFE. -- NOW FOR THE DEMONSTRATION!
JOR-L REACHES FOR THE SWITCH WHICH WILL LAUNCH THE MODEL SPACE-SHIP UPON ITS MOMENTOUS FLIGHT ACROSS SPACE TO EARTH!

Superman—By Jerry Siegel and Joe Shuster *Destruction!* (Copyright, 1939.)

AS JOR-L IS ABOUT TO TOUCH THE SWITCH'S HANDLE, HE IS FLUNG OFF-BALANCE BY A SUDDEN LURCHING OF THE ROOF . . . .
EARTHQUAKE!
LOOK --THE GROUND --- HEAVING -- PARTING -- FLAMING --
THE END HAS COME SOONER THAN I EXPECTED!
NOT A SECOND TO LOSE! THE MODEL-FLIER WILL HOLD ONE OF US!
IF ONLY ONE CAN ESCAPE, THEN IT MUST BE OUR CHILD!

Superman—By Jerry Siegel and Joe Shuster *Speeding Towards Earth* (Copyright, 1939.)

UP -- UP FROM JOR-L'S LABORATORY STREAKS THE ROCKET-SHIP BEARING KAL-L FROM CERTAIN DESTRUCTION
AN INSTANT AFTER THEIR GLORIOUS, SELF-SACRIFICING GESTURE, JOR-L AND LORA PERISH IN THE EARTH QUAKE'S AWFUL GRIP!
AND IN STILL ANOTHER INSTANT, THE TREMENDOUS PLANET OF KRYPTON EXPLODES INTO A MILLION FRAGMENTS!
ROCKED BY THE EXPLOSION, BUT ESCAPING ANNIHILATION, THE LITTLE ROCKET-VESSEL CONTINUES ON ITS WAY TO EARTH... ITS CARGO, THE SOLE SURVIVOR OF A ONCE MIGHTY CIVILIZATION!
10

Superman—By Jerry Siegel and Joe Shuster *A Perilous Arrival* (Copyright, 1939.)

PERIL AFTER PERIL IS NARROWLY AVOIDED BY THE ROCKETING SPACE-FLIER! -- A GREAT JAGGED METEOR . . .
. . . THE GRAVITY OF A GIANT SUN ALMOST DRAWS THE VESSEL TO A MOLTEN DEATH . . . !
SAFETY APPEARS TO HAVE AT LAST BEEN REACHED, WHEN IT FINALLY STREAKS DOWN INTO EARTH'S ATMOSPHERE . . .
BUT DUE TO FRICTION WITH THE AIR, THE SHIP TAKES FIRE UPON LANDING -- HUNGRY FLAMES CREEP GREEDILY TOWARD THE TINY SLEEPING PASSENGER . . . !
11

Superman—By Jerry Siegel and Joe Shuster *The Superman Is Here!* (Copyright, 1939.)

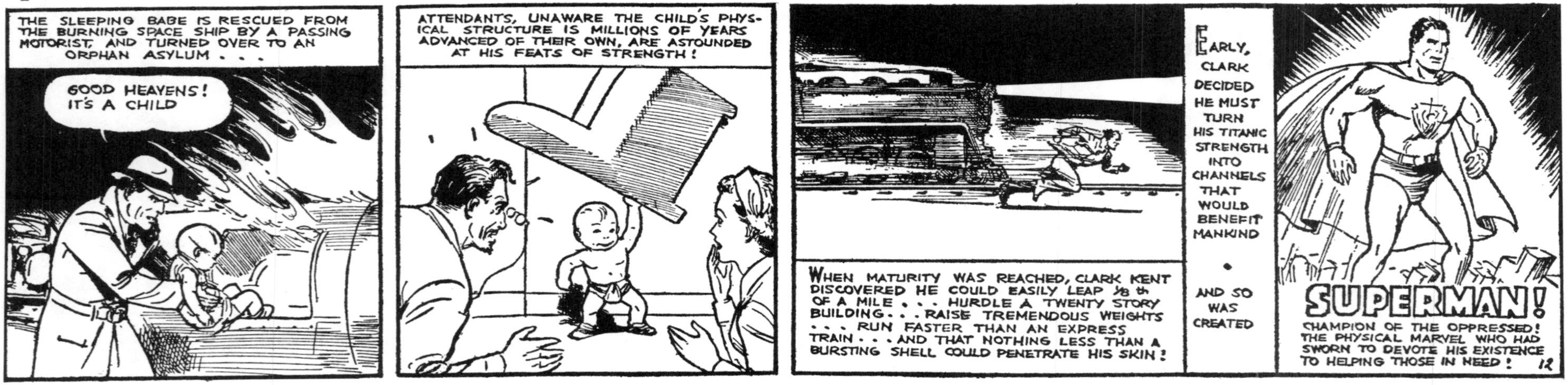
THE SLEEPING BABE IS RESCUED FROM THE BURNING SPACE SHIP BY A PASSING MOTORIST, AND TURNED OVER TO AN ORPHAN ASYLUM . . .
GOOD HEAVENS! IT'S A CHILD
ATTENDANTS, UNAWARE THE CHILD'S PHYSICAL STRUCTURE IS MILLIONS OF YEARS ADVANCED OF THEIR OWN, ARE ASTOUNDED AT HIS FEATS OF STRENGTH!
WHEN MATURITY WAS REACHED, CLARK KENT DISCOVERED HE COULD EASILY LEAP 1/8 th OF A MILE . . . HURDLE A TWENTY STORY BUILDING . . . RAISE TREMENDOUS WEIGHTS . . . RUN FASTER THAN AN EXPRESS TRAIN . . . AND THAT NOTHING LESS THAN A BURSTING SHELL COULD PENETRATE HIS SKIN!
EARLY, CLARK DECIDED HE MUST TURN HIS TITANIC STRENGTH INTO CHANNELS THAT WOULD BENEFIT MANKIND
AND SO WAS CREATED
SUPERMAN!
CHAMPION OF THE OPPRESSED! THE PHYSICAL MARVEL WHO HAD SWORN TO DEVOTE HIS EXISTENCE TO HELPING THOSE IN NEED!
12

EPISODE TWO
WAR ON CRIME

Superman—By Jerry Siegel and Joe Shuster *To the Rescue.* (Copyright, 1939.)

STAR
EXTRA
TEN MEN TRAPPED IN STEEL VAULT!
FIEND RESPONSIBLE
NICK RICO
FACE DEATH BY SUFFOCATION
EARLY THIS MORNING, TEN EMPLOYEES OF THE FIRST NATIONAL BANK WERE SEALED WITHIN THE BANK'S STEEL VAULT BY BANDITS WHO HAD RANSACKED ITS CONTENTS.
DUE TO ITS TIME-LOCK MECHANISM, THE VAULT'S MASSIVE DOORS WILL NOT SWING OPEN FOR SEVERAL HOURS.
MEANWHILE, ARMED WITH ACETYLENE-TORCHES, RESCUERS SEEK TO BATTER THEIR WAY TO THE ENTRAPPED MEN'S AID.
SORRY TO BURST IN LIKE THIS, GENTLEMEN!
W-WHO--? --W-WHAT--?
POLICE! HELP!!
NEXT INSTANT THE CLOAKED FIGURE LEAPS AT THE BANK VAULT-- AN EAR-SPLITTING RENDING AND CRASHING-- BEFORE HIS ATTACK THE STEEL CRUMPLES AS THO IT WERE MERE PUTTY!
J-JUMPING JUPITER! —I'M SEEING THINGS! THIS CAN'T BE— IT CAN'T!
BUT— IT—IS!!
13.

Superman—By Jerry Siegel and Joe Shuster *Just in Time* (Copyright, 1939.)

SAVED! -- BUT HOW DID --?
SORRY I CAN'T REMAIN TO ANSWER THAT!
SHORTLY LATER... ABOVE THE CITY!
NOW TO HURRY BACK TO MY APARTMENT AND SEE WHAT THE NEWSPAPERS SAY!
THE WORLD IS JUBILANT AS NEWS OF THE CLERKS' RESCUE IS SPREAD...
DAILY STAR
EXTR
CLERKS SAVED
RESCUE DETAILS NOT CLEAR
TWO DEAD
McClure Newspaper Syndicate
BUT CLARK KENT, AS HE REMOVES HIS SUPERMAN COSTUME, THINKS SADLY OF THE TWO CLERKS WHO DIED
I MUST BECOME A REPORTER -- GET NEWS FLASHES PROMPTLY -- SO THAT THIS WILL NEVER OCCUR AGAIN!
14.
AND SO IS DETERMINED A DECISION FATED TO CHANGE THE DESTINY OF A WORLD !

uperman—By Jerry Siegel and Joe Shuster *A Strange Visitor* (Copyright, 1939.)

EDITORIAL OFFICE OF THE DAILY STAR, A PROGRESSIVE NEWSPAPER . . .
BUT BOSS! — YOU CAN'T. . . YOU SIMPLY MUSN'T DISCONTINUE MY GRAFT EXPOSE' SERIES NOW! WHY IN A FEW DAYS I'LL BE ABLE TO REVEAL THE NAME OF THE LEADER BEHIND THE ENTIRE MESS!
O.K. LOIS! — I'LL GIVE YOU A LITTLE MORE TIME. BUT I WARN YOU! NAME HIM SOON OR IT'S BACK TO THE LOVELORN COLUMN FOR YOU!
THO HE IS SEATED IN THE ADJOINING OFFICE, CLARK'S SUPER-SENSITIVE EARS HAVE CAUGHT EVERY WORD!
("—THAT GIRL HAS SPUNK! -- SAY! WHO'S THIS? LOOKS LIKE AN UNDERWORLD RAT TO ME! —")
AS LOIS EMERGES FROM THE EDITOR'S OFFICE, SHE SURREPTITIOUSLY SIGNALS THE FURTIVE STRANGER TO FOLLOW HER
("—NOW WHY WOULD A SWEET LOOKING KID LIKE HER HAVE ANYTHING TO DO WITH A TOUGH MUG LIKE HIM...
DAILY
CITY EDITOR
YOU MAY SEE THE EDITOR NOW, SIR.
("—I'D MUCH RATHER SEE WHAT THOSE TWO ARE UP TO—")

Superman—By Jerry Siegel and Joe Shuster *Superman Gets a Job* (Copyright, 1939.)

TO FORESTALL ANY POSSIBLE FUTURE SUSPICION OF HIS TRUE IDENTITY AS SUPERMAN, CLARK KENT HAS ADOPTED GLASSES AND AN ASSUMED ATTITUDE OF MEEKNESS.
I--ER--THAT IS--I'D LIKE TO APPLY FOR THE POSITION OF REPORTER
YOU WOULD, EH? AND I SUPPOSE, LIKE ALL THE OTHER BY-LINE-STRUCK GALOOTS WHO WASTE MY TIME, YOU'VE HAD ABSOLUTELY NO EXPERIENCE!
THO APPARENTLY LISTENING TO THE EDITOR, CLARK'S SUPER-ACUTE EARS ARE EAVESDROPPING ON A CONVERSATION IN A DISTANT ROOM.
HERE YOU ARE, "WEASEL": $40! —NOW I WANT ONLY ONE MORE BIT OF INFORMATION FROM YOU.-- WHO IS THE 'BIG BOSS' BEHIND THE GRAFT AT CITY HALL?
TH' 'BIG BOSS'! —LADY! HE'S DYNAMITE! —IT'LL COST YA 500 SMACKERS FER THAT INFO'! HAVE TH' DOUGH READY T'MORRA NIGHT.
I'VE FOUND THAT THE ONLY WAY TO RID MYSELF OF FELLOWS LIKE YOU IS TO GIVE THEM AN IMPOSSIBLE TEST ASSIGNMENT. —SAY, ARE YOU LISTENING TO ME?
CERTAINLY-- WHAT'S MY ASSIGNMENT?
THERE'S A SILLY RUMOR CIRCULATING ABOUT TOWN THAT A MAN NAMED SUPERMAN, WHO IS POSSESSED OF GIGANTIC STRENGTH, ACTUALLY EXISTS. I'D LIKE YOU TO INTERVIEW HIM FOR THE DAILY STAR. THINK YOU CAN DO IT?
LISTEN, PAL! —IF I CAN'T FIND OUT ANYTHING ABOUT SUPERMAN NO ONE CAN!

Superman—By Jerry Siegel and Joe Shuster

His First Assignment

(Copyright, 1939.)

OUTSIDE CLARK KENT REMOVES GLASSES AND OUTER GARMENTS, TRANSFORMING HIMSELF INTO THE DYNAMIC SUPERMAN!
HERE HE COMES NOW!
17
..ONE MOMENT, "WEASEL"! WHO IS THE "BIG BOSS" BEHIND THE GRAFTING AT CITY HALL?
I DONT KNOW WOT YER TALKIN' ABOUT! -- LEGGO MY HAND!
YOUR FOOT WILL DO JUST AS WELL!
..MAYBE A BIRD'S-EYE VIEW OF THINGS WILL MAKE YOU FEEL LIKE TALKING, EH, "WEASEL"?
HALP!
SEIZING "WEASEL" ABOUT THE MIDDLE, SUPERMAN LEAPS TO A TELEPHONE WIRE FAR ABOVE THE CITY! (CONT'D)

Superman—By Jerry Siegel and Joe Shuster

The Third Degree

(Copyright, 1939.)

IN AN EFFORT TO FIND OUT WHO IS THE "BIG BOSS" BEHIND THE GRAFTING IN THE CITY HALL, SUPERMAN IS GIVING THE "WEASEL" THE THIRD DEGREE IN HIS OWN INIMITABLE WAY......... HUNDREDS OF FEET ABOVE THE CITY STREETS..
WELL.. HOW ABOUT IT WEASEL? ARE YOU GOING TO FESS UP AND TELL POPPA ALL ABOUT IT?
NO! NO! IF I TALK DEY'LL TAKE ME FER A RIDE!
ALL RIGHT, PALSY WALSY-- ..MAYBE YOU'D RATHER GO FOR A NICE LITTLE RIDE WITH ME!
YEOW! DE GUY'S NUTS!
18
HOW DOES SUPERMAN DO IT? THE FOLLOWING IS A SCIENTIFIC EXPLANATION OF HIS AMAZING STRENGTH ----
HE HAD COME FROM A PLANET WHOSE INHABITANTS' PHYSICAL STRUCTURE WAS MILLIONS OF YEARS ADVANCED OF OUR OWN. UPON REACHING MATURITY, THE PEOPLE OF HIS RACE BECAME GIFTED WITH TITANIC STRENGTH!
--INCREDIBLE? NO! FOR EVEN TODAY ON OUR WORLD EXIST CREATURES WITH SUPER-STRENGTH!
THE LOWLY ANT CAN SUPPORT WEIGHTS HUNDREDS OF TIMES ITS OWN.
THE GRASSHOPPER LEAPS WHAT TO MAN WOULD BE THE SPACE OF SEVERAL CITY BLOCKS.
AND SO, SUPERMAN, WITH HIS EXTRAORDINARY POWERS, CONTINUES ENTHUSIASTICALLY TO BREAK DOWN "THE WEASEL'S" RESISTANCE. DON'T MISS THE NEXT EPISODE!!!

Superman—By Jerry Siegel and Joe Shuster

Superman in Action

(Copyright, 1939.)

FORWARD RACES *SUPERMAN*, IN RECKLESS ABANDON. . . .
STOP! STOP! -- WE'LL BE ELECTROCUTED!
NO, WE WON'T! BIRDS SIT ON TELEPHONE WIRES AND *THEY* AREN'T ELECTROCUTED--
--NOT UNLESS THEY TOUCH A TELEPHONE-POLE AND ARE GROUNDED! --OOPS! JUST MISSED THAT POLE!
HM-MM! — I WONDER IF WE COULD JUMP ALL THE WAY TO THAT BUILDING?
NO! — DON'T!
DESPITE 'WEASEL'S SHRIEKED PROTESTS, *SUPERMAN* LEAPS OUTWARD . . . .
MISSED-- DOGGONE IT!
TO BE CONTINUED—

Superman—By Jerry Siegel and Joe Shuster

Superman Makes Him Talk

(Copyright, 1939.)

DID YOU EVER WONDER HOW IT WOULD FEEL TO FALL A GREAT DISTANCE AND BE CRUSHED TO A PULP?
SOME FUN! — LET'S DO IT AGAIN!
AGAIN? -- NO! I'LL TALK! — TH' MAN YOU WANT IS JACK MARTIN TH' POLITICAL BOSS!
MARTIN, EH? -- I THINK I'LL PAY HIM A VISIT!
BUT AT THAT VERY MOMENT. . .
THAT'S HER, MARTIN! LOIS LANE, TH' GIRL WHO HAS SWORN TO EXPOSE YOU!
HERE'S A GAT. YOU KNOW WHAT TO DO!

Superman—By Jerry Siegel and Joe Shuster *A Little Gun Play* (Copyright, 1939.)

WARN TH' BOSS, NICKY! — HE'S GONNA BE VISITED BY *TH' MOST DANGEROUS MAN ALIVE!*
DON'T WORRY, "WEASEL"! -- ME AN' TH' BOYS WILL ARRANGE A LI'L RECEPTION FER HIM!
21
WHERE'S MARTIN ?
ALL RIGHT, BOYS! — *LET 'IM HAVE IT!*
OUT FROM BEHIND HIDDEN PANELS STEP ARMED MEN
NEXT INSTANT *SUPERMAN* IS THE TARGET OF A DEAFENING BARRAGE!
L-LOOK!
HE WON'T DIE!!
GLAD I CAN'T SAY THE SAME FOR YOU!

Superman—By Jerry Siegel and Joe Shuster *Is Superman Late?* (Copyright, 1939.)

SUPERMAN NEATLY WRAPS THE MACHINE-GUNS AROUND THE THUGS' NECKS . . .
YOU BOYS OUGHT TO SEE ME SOME TIME WHEN I *REALLY* GET SORE!
WILL YOU TELL ME WHERE MARTIN IS OR MUST I --!
HE'S GONE TO TH' *DAILY* TO QUIET THAT GIRL REPORTER!
LEAPING HIGH ABOVE THE CITY, THE MAN OF STEEL FOCUSES HIS TELESCOPIC VISION UPON THE DISTANT NEWSPAPER BUILDING . . .
OH-OH! — WHAT'S THIS ?
WHAT *SUPERMAN* SAW . . . . !
INTO THAT CAR, QUICK, BEFORE I PLUG YA!
22

Superman—By Jerry Siegel and Joe Shuster

Superman—Super Strength

(Copyright, 1939.)

WITH LOIS HIS PRISONER, MARTIN SPEEDS TOWARD HIS WAITING PLANE IN A HIDDEN FIELD JUST OUTSIDE THE CITY. SUDDENLY
.....AS THEY APPROACH THE FLYING FIELD...
SOME ONE'S IN TH' CENTER OF TH' ROAD! —HA! HA! WATCH ME SCARE HIM STIFF!
LOOK OUT!! YOU'LL HIT HIM!
SUPERMAN GRASPS THE BUMPER OF THE ONRUSHING AUTOMOBILE AND FORCES IT TO A DEAD STOP!!!
STEP ON IT, BOSS...! RUN HIM DOWN!!
HOLY CATS! I CAN'T! HE'S HOLDIN' US!!
WITH ONE HAND SUPERMAN LIFTS—THE CAR HIGH ABOVE HIS HEAD AND SHAKES OUT ITS ASTOUNDED OCCUPANTS; WITH THE OTHER HE CATCHES LOIS-

Superman—By Jerry Siegel and Joe Shuster

Flying Through Space

(Copyright, 1939.)

WHILE SUPERMAN DEMOLISHES THE CAR, MARTIN REGAINS CONCIOUSNESS, AND DRAGS LOIS TOWARDS HIS WAITING PLANE-----
GO ON-- GET IN!
LET ME GO!!
FORCING HER IN, THEY HURRIEDLY TAKE OFF--
YOU LET ME GO!
LOOK OUT, YOU LITTLE FOOL--- YOU'LL FALL OUT!!!
EEEEEEEE
TRYING TO ESCAPE THE EVIL POLITICIAN'S GRASP, LOIS FALLS OUT OF THE PLANE AND PLUMMETS DOWN TOWARD...WHAT?

Superman—By Jerry Siegel and Joe Shuster *Aerial Activities* (Copyright, 1939.)

SIGHTING LOIS FALLING, SUPERMAN LEAPS . . . .
IF I CAN ONLY MAKE IT!
GOT HER!
25
WHEN THEY STRIKE EARTH . . .
W-WHAT KIND OF CREATURE ARE YOU?
YOU NEEDN'T BE AFRAID! I WON'T HARM YOU! --BUT AS FOR THOSE COWARDLY KILLERS . .!!
COME AND GET IT!
TO THE ATTACK SPRINGS SUPERMAN!! FOR THE FIRST TIME IN HISTORY, MAN AND PLANE MEET IN SINGLEHANDED BATTLE!

Superman—By Jerry Siegel and Joe Shuster *Unwelcome Passenger* (Copyright, 1939.)

AS THE CROOKED POLITICIAN'S PLANE SWOOPS BY, IT SEEKS TO VEER AWAY FROM THE MAN OF STEEL . . .
WHOA! — YOU ALMOST FORGOT ME!
DESPERATELY, THE PLANE LOOPS . . . WHIRLS . . . ZOOMS . . .
RIDE 'IM COWBOY!
26
HE'S REACHED THE WINGS! — THROW HIM OFF!!
I CAN'T! —HE AIN'T HUMAN!

Superman—By Jerry Siegel and Joe Shuster *Victory and Danger.* (Copyright, 1939.)

CLINGING TO THE PLANE WITH BULL-DOG TENACITY, SUPERMAN RIPS AND TEARS ITS WING TO SHREDS!
RIP
27
DOWN HURTLES THE STRICKEN VESSEL -- DOWN, DOWN TO A CRUSHING DOOM . . .
TERRORIZED BY THE INCREDIBLE DRAMA IN THE SKIES, LOIS RUNS BLINDLY, FEAR-CRAZED, UNSEEING, UNTIL SHE BLUNDERS INTO . . .
QUICKSAND! HELP!

Superman—By Jerry Siegel and Joe Shuster *Safe Again* (Copyright, 1939.)

WHAT'S THAT? A SCREAM!
28
COMING!
O-OOH – YOU'RE... HURTING ME!
I'LL HAVE YOU FREE IN A SECOND!
SUPER-STRENGTH VERSUS TENACIOUS QUICKSAND! DESPITE THE BOG'S RELENTLESS GRIP, SUPERMAN BATTLES HIS WAY OUT... STEP-BY-STEP...

Superman—By Jerry Siegel and Joe Shuster — *On Time* — (Copyright, 1939.)

HOLD ME TIGHT! — I'M AFRAID!
I'LL BE DELIGHTED!
FIGHTING HIS WAY FREE OF THE TREACHEROUS QUICKSAND, SUPERMAN BEGINS A RETURN JOURNEY TO THE CITY.
© 1939, McClure Newspaper Syndicate
29
EDITORIAL ROOM OF THE DAILY . . .
WHERE IN BLAZES IS LOIS LANE? — WE GO TO PRESS IN FIVE MINUTES!
MAY I ASSIST YOU? HERE'S LOIS LANE -- A TRIFLE SCARED BUT STILL LOIS LANE!
WHAT-- ???

Superman—By Jerry Siegel and Joe Shuster — *His Reward* — (Copyright, 1939.)

SO-LONG! — BETTER STICK TO THE LOVELORN COLUMN FROM NOW ON . . . IT'S SAFER!
STOP HIM! -- HE'S SUPERMAN!
SUPERMAN! — JUMPIN' CATFISH!
WAIT! HOW ABOUT AN INTERVIEW?
YOU'LL HAVE TO SEE CLARK KENT ABOUT THAT! -- GOODBY, NOW!
LATER — WHEN CLARK RETURNS TO THE NEWSPAPER OFFICE . . .
YOU MEAN. . . I'M HIRED . . !
EXACTLY! — I DON'T KNOW HOW YOU GOT THAT SUPERMAN INTERVIEW, BUT LET'S HAVE IT!
30
SUPERMAN
MAN OF STEEL
begins A STARTLING NEW ADVENTURE MONDAY
DONT MISS IT!

EPISODE THREE

THE COMEBACK OF LARRY TRENT

©NE EVENING, WHILE OUT SEARCHING FOR SOMEONE IN NEED OF ASSISTANCE, SUPERMAN SIGHTS . . .
SOMEONE'S FALLING!
ALMOST MISSED!
DOWN STREAK THE TWO FIGURES . . . DELIBERATELY, SUPERMAN RECEIVES THE BRUNT OF THE SHOCK WHEN THEY STRIKE WATER . . . .
1939, McClure Newspaper Syndicate
LATER . . . WHEN THEY REACH SHORE
HE'S REVIVING! — HIS FACE . . . IT LOOKS FAMILIAR . . . AND YET, I CAN'T RECALL WHO HE IS!
31

WH-WHERE-- W-WHO--?
I SAVED YOU FROM FALLING TO YOUR DEATH. -- WHAT IS YOUR NAME? I'VE SEEN YOU BEFORE, BUT YOUR EXACT IDENTITY HAS SLIPPED MY MEMORY!
WHOA! IS THAT THE WAY FOR YOU TO BEHAVE TOWARD THE MAN WHO SAVED YOUR LIFE?
FOOL! I WAS COM-MITTING SUICIDE!
IN A FURY, THE MAN ATTACKS SUPERMAN.
I'LL TEACH YOU TO INTERFERE IN OTHER PEOPLES LIVES!
SAY, YOU CERTAINLY CAN HANDLE YOUR DUKES! — COULD YOU BE . . ?
32 1939, McClure Newspaper Syndicate
I'VE GOT IT! -- YOU'RE LARRY TRENT, EX-HEAVY-WEIGHT CHAMPION OF THE WORLD!

SO THAT'S WHO YOU ARE! LARRY TRENT, EX-HEAVY-WEIGHT CHAMP OF THE WORLD! — WHAT-EVER DROVE YOU TO SUICIDE?
I'VE LOST ALL FAITH IN PEOPLE AND MYSELF. THERE'S NOTHING TO LIVE FOR!
LARRY'S STORY OF HIS DOWN-FALL
"MY CROOKED MANAGER WORKED HAND-IN-GLOVE WITH RUTHLESS GANGSTERS."
GET IT? LARRY TRENT LOSES THE CHAMPIONSHIP AND YOU GET CUT IN ON TH' HEAVY BETTINGS -- BUT IF HE WINS . . .
DON'T WORRY. TH' BOY REFUSES TO TAKE A DIVE BUT LEAVE IT TO ME!
1939 McClure Newspaper Syndicate
"ON THE NIGHT OF THE BIG FIGHT, HE PLACED A DRUG IN MY DRINK."
"MY SENSES REELING FROM THE EFFECTS OF THE DRUG, I WAS KAYOED -- LOST MY TITLE."
I'VE GONE STEADILY DOWN SINCE THEN, UNTIL NOW I'M A STUMBLE-BUM, FIGHTING FOR $5 A NIGHT . . . WHEN I CAN GET IT. . -- I WISH YOU HAD LET ME DIE!
33

IF I WERE TO RESTORE THE TITLE TO YOU, WOULD IT BRING BACK YOUR SELF-RESPECT?
WOULD IT!! -- BUT WHAT COULD YOU POSSIBLY DO?
DISGUISE MYSELF AS YOU, AND BATTLE MY WAY TO THE HEAVYWEIGHT CHAMPION-SHIP OF THE WORLD!
YOU CRAZY LOON! -- NO SOONER WOULD YOU ENTER THE RING THEN YOU'D BE KNOCKED COLD!
BUT IF I WERE TO EXERCISE REGULARLY, SURELY I COULD BUILD UP MY STRENGTH TO EQUAL THAT OF PROFESSIONAL FIGHTERS!
YOU POOR SAP! — IT WOULD TAKE YOU YEARS!
IN THAT CASE I'D BETTER BEGIN RIGHT NOW!!
1939, McClure Newspaper Syndicate
34

NOW DO YOU BELIEVE I'VE A CHANCE FOR THE HEAVYWEIGHT TITLE OF THE WORLD?
OF THE WORLD? GOOD LORD! -- OF THE UNIVERSE!
THEN YOU'RE WILLING TO CO-OPERATE WITH ME?
YOU BET! BOY! IF I STICK WITH YOU, I'M REALLY GOING PLACES!
HEY! WHAT TH'—!
— DON'T BE ALARMED!
1939, McClure Newspaper Syndicate
35
WE'RE GOING PLACES, ALL RIGHT, LARRY, BUT SHOOTING JUST A LITTLE HIGHER THAN YOU EXPECTED!

DOWN STREAKS SUPERMAN TOWARD THE WINDOW-SILL OF AN APARTMENT HE HAS RENTED FOR EMERGENCIES . . .
THIS IS WHERE YOU'LL STAY FOR THE NEXT SEVERAL MONTHS!
1939 McClure Newspaper Syndicate
WHERE WERE YOU TO HAVE FOUGHT NEXT?
THE CRYSTAL CLUB -- TONIGHT!
GIVE ME SOME POINTERS ABOUT THE PEOPLE YOU KNOW!
APPLYING MAKE-UP, SUPERMAN EXPERTLY ALTERS THE APPEARANCE OF HIS FEATURES
SHORTLY AFTER
GOOD GOSH! — YOU'RE ME!
WRONG! YOU'RE NOT LOOKING AT LARRY TRENT, EX-CHAMP . . . BUT AT LARRY TRENT, THE COMING CHAMPION OF THE WORLD!

DISGUISED AS LARRY TRENT, SUPERMAN ENTERS THE REAR OF THE CRYSTAL CLUB
GET OVER THERE WITH THE OTHERS, TRENT!
OKAY, BOSS.
1939, McClure Newspaper Syndicate
NOW LISTEN, YOU MUGS, I WANT ACTION, SEE? AND PLENTY OF LAUGHS! —NOW GET INTO THE RING AND WHEN I GIVE THE SIGNAL, START SOCKIN'!
LADIES AND GENTLEMEN, YOU'RE ABOUT TO WITNESS TWELVE MEN BATTLING TOGETHER IN ONE RING! NOW I ASK YA: IS THAT GIVIN' YOU YER MONEY'S WORTH? IS IT?
LET 'EM LOOSE!
HOO-RAY!
37
BONG
TOMORROW'S RELEASE OCCURS EXACTLY ONE SECOND LATER

AT THE SOUND OF THE BELL, SUPERMAN IS OFF LIKE A STREAKING ARROW!
FASTER THAN THE EYE CAN FOLLOW, HE CLIPS ELEVEN EXPOSED JAWS!
REALLY!— THIS IS TOO SIMPLE!
WHAM
1939, McClure Newspaper Syndicate
39
AND WITHIN THE SPACE OF ONE SECOND . . .
?
!
. . . IS THE ONLY CONSCIOUS BATTLER LEFT IN THE RING!
GOT ANY MORE?

TH' WINNER!
JUMPIN' JITTERBUGS, LARRY, SEE JOCK KANE, TH' FAMOUS FIGHT PROMOTER AN' SAY I SENT YOU! — — KID, YOU'LL BE A SENSATION AGAIN!
THANKS.
1939, McClure Newspaper Syndicate
LATER . . . THE MAN OF STEEL'S APARTMENT — — AS SUPERMAN SPARS WITH LARRY TRENT . . .
AND SO I WAS TOLD TO VISIT JOCK KANE!
KANE? — EVER SINCE I LOST THE TITLE, I'VE BEEN THAT GUY'S PET HATE!
39
SOMEHOW, I'VE A HUNCH MR. KANE IS GOING TO CHANGE HIS ATTITUDE!
TCH! TCH! — YOU LEFT YOURSELF WIDE OPEN THAT TIME, TRENT!

NEXT MORNING, DISGUISED AS TRENT, SUPERMAN CALLS ON KANE . . .
CHARLIE BENNETT SENT ME. HE THOUGHT YOU MIGHT ARRANGE A FIGHT FOR ME, AGAIN!
HEAR THAT, "SLUGGER"?
TH' GUY'S SLAP-HAPPY!
LISTEN, YOU BROKEN-DOWN BUM OF A HAS-BEEN, WE GOT NO USE FOR TRASH AROUND HERE! — — CLEAR OUT!
BUT CHARLIE SAID . . .
(— WAIT, JOCK! STALL FOR TIME WHILE I RIB TH' DUMB CLUCK!
(— HO! HO! — I GET IT! TH' "HOT FOOT!")
THIS IS GONNA BE FUNNY!
1939, McClure Newspaper Syndicate.
40
EVEN FUNNIER THAN YOU EXPECT, "SLUGGER"!

SUPERMAN IS UNAWARE HE IS GETTING THE "HOT-FOOT" UNTIL--
("-WHAT TH'-! DON'T HE EVEN FEEL IT?-")
--"SLUGGER" BURNS HIS OWN FINGERS!
OUCH! -MY FINGER!
?
PRACTICAL JOKER, EH? —LAUGH THIS OFF!!
1939, McClure Newspaper Syndicate
41
GOOD GRIEF, TRENT! YOU'VE KNOCKED OUT "SLUGGER" DOLAN, ONE OF TH' TOUGHEST FIGHTERS IN TH' GAME!
FOR A TOUGH GUY, HE'S GOT A MIGHTY SOFT CHIN!

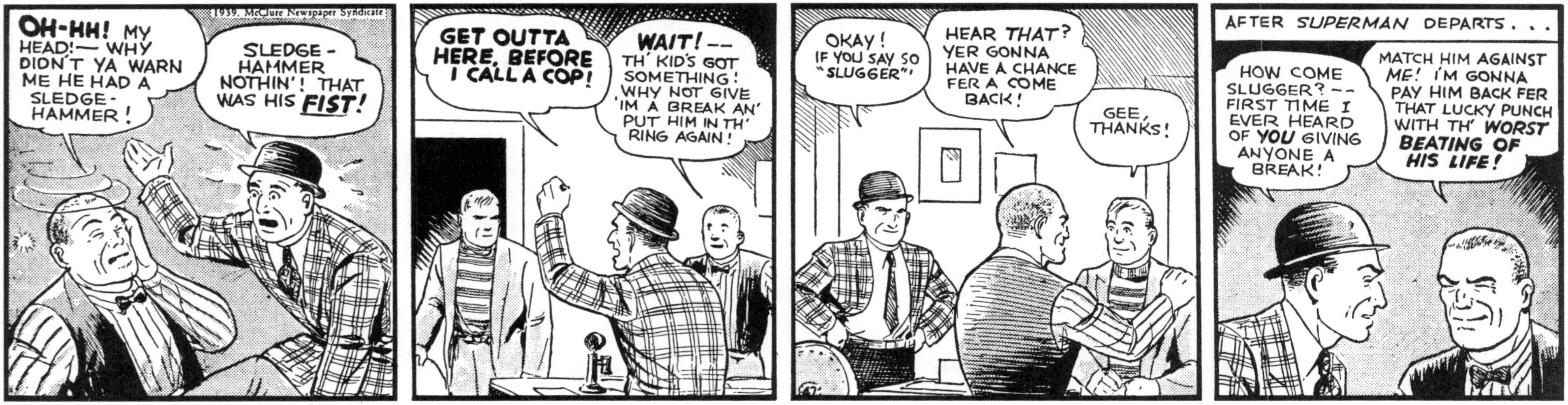
1939, McClure Newspaper Syndicate
OH-HH! MY HEAD!— WHY DIDN'T YA WARN ME HE HAD A SLEDGE-HAMMER!
SLEDGE-HAMMER NOTHIN'! THAT WAS HIS FIST!
GET OUTTA HERE, BEFORE I CALL A COP!
WAIT!-- TH' KID'S GOT SOMETHING! WHY NOT GIVE 'IM A BREAK AN' PUT HIM IN TH' RING AGAIN!
OKAY! IF YOU SAY SO "SLUGGER"!
HEAR THAT? YER GONNA HAVE A CHANCE FER A COME BACK!
GEE, THANKS!
AFTER SUPERMAN DEPARTS...
HOW COME SLUGGER?-- FIRST TIME I EVER HEARD OF YOU GIVING ANYONE A BREAK!
MATCH HIM AGAINST ME! I'M GONNA PAY HIM BACK FER THAT LUCKY PUNCH WITH TH' WORST BEATING OF HIS LIFE!

ANY LUCK?
I'VE LANDED A MATCH WITH "SLUGGER" BARNES —ARE YOU READY FOR YOUR DAILY WORK-OUT, LARRY?
AW, WHAT'S TH' USE? I'LL NEVER GET BACK INTO GOOD CONDITION ANYWAY!
SO, YOU WON'T FIGHT EH?
1939, McClure Newspaper Syndicate
WHAT YOU NEED IS A LITTLE ENCOURAGE-MENT!
WHY, YOU—! (SPLUTTER)
BLAST YA!— I'LL MOW YA DOWN!
IT WORKED!

THE EVENING OF THE BARNES VS. TRENT FIGHT -- OUTSIDE THE ARENA...
I'VE GOT TO HURRY TO MY DRESSING-ROOM NOW -- SEE YOU LATER, LARRY!
IT'S GONNA BE A FUNNY SENSATION -- WATCHIN' MYSELF BATTLIN' IN THE RING!
EXIT
WELL, KID! IN A FEW MINUTES WE'LL BE SLUGGIN' AWAY!
THANKS FOR DROPPIN' IN TO WISH ME LUCK, BARNES
LUCK, NOTHIN'! I'M GONNA BEAT YOU SO BAD, YOU'LL WISH YA NEVER SAW A PAIR OF BOXIN' GLOVES!
YEAH? WELL, I KNOCKED YOU COLD ONCE -- AND HISTORY HAS BEEN KNOWN TO REPEAT ITSELF!
LATER—AT THE SOUND OF THE GONG THE TWO LEAP AT EACH OTHER LIKE UNLEASHED JUNGLE BEASTS! -- THE BATTLE IS ON!
1939, McClure Newspaper Syndicate

BARNES SLAMS A TERRIFIC LEFT TO SUPERMAN'S JAW!
HERE'S THAT PUNCH BACK... WITH INTEREST!
NEXT INSTANT, HAVING STRUCK A CHIN AS UNYIELDING AS STEEL, HE YOWLS WITH PAIN!
YEEOW
WHAT IN--??
I'LL--!
TCH! TCH! MUSTN'T LOSE YOUR TEMPER!
GOSH, IT'S WARM HERE! KEEP UP THE FANNING MAYBE IT'LL COOL ME OFF!
45
1939, McClure Newspaper Syndicate

EACH TIME BARNES STRIKES SUPERMAN IT FEELS TO HIM AS THO HE WERE BATTERING A STONE WALL!
OUCH! WHAT TH'--?
IN THE AUDIENCE LARRY TRENT CHEERS FOR... HIMSELF!
ATTABOY, LARRY! KNOCK THE STUFFIN'S OUTTA HIM!
BARNES' FRANTIC BLOWS ONLY WEAR HIMSELF DOWN...
(PUFF!— PUFF!)
I'M STILL WAITING FOR THAT BAD BEATING YOU PROMISED ME!
1939, McClure Newspaper Syndicate
...UNTIL ONE OF HIS FLAILING HAYMAKERS KNOCKS HIM OUT!
46

-- EIGHT, NINE, TEN! YOU'RE OUT!!
47 © 1939, McClure Newspaper Syndicate
AND SO IT IS THAT SUPERMAN, IN THE GUISE OF LARRY TRENT, WINS THE MATCH TO EVERYONE'S ASTONISHMENT!
YOU CHEAP BUM! YOU SAID YOU WERE GOIN' TO KNOCK HIM FOR A LOOP!
BOO BOO
I CAN'T UNDERSTAND IT! -- I STILL CAN'T UNDERSTAND IT!
BOO
ARE YOU GOING TO MAKE ANOTHER TRY FOR THE HEAVYWEIGHT TITLE, TRENT?
NOPE! NOT JUST A "TRY"... I'M GOING TO GET IT!

WHEN SUPERMAN REACHES HIS DRESSING ROOM....
WAIT, LARRY! I WANT TO TALK TO YOU!
AND WHO ARE YOU?
I DON'T BLAME YOU FOR SLIGHTING YOUR OLD MANAGER. BUT LISTEN, KID! I BUILT YOU UP TO TH' TOP OF TH' HEAP, ONCE -- AND I CAN DO IT AGAIN!
SUPERMAN REALIZES HE IS TALKING TO TOM CROY, LARRY'S FORMER CROOKED MANAGER...
WELL, WHAT DO YOU SAY?
OKAY, TOM!
© 1939, McClure Newspaper Syndicate
48
SMART LAD! YOU'LL NEVER REGRET THIS! ("—HO! HO! DID I PUT THAT OVER!—")
I'M SURE I WON'T! ("—BUT YOU'LL REGRET IT!—")

49
HO! HO! — DID I PUT THAT ONE OVER NEATLY!
HOW D' YA MAKE OUT?
IT WAS A CINCH! YOU SHOULD'VE SEEN HOW EASILY I ROPED HIM IN!
THE SAP'S GOT ABSOLUTELY NO IDEA WE'RE GONNA PULL TH' SAME STUNT AGAIN -- BUILD HIM UP TO MEET TH' CHAMP, THEN GIVE HIM A DRUGGED DRINK BEFORE TH' FIGHT AN' CLEAN UP BETTIN'!
FROM ATOP A NEARBY BUILDING, SUPERMAN'S SUPER-ACUTE HEARING HAS ENABLED HIM TO HEAR EVERY WORD
JUST AS I SUSPECTED!
1939. McClure Newspaper Syndicate
LATER — EDITORIAL OFFICE OF THE DAILY STAR . . .
THIS STORY YOU'VE WRITTEN PREDICTING A COMEBACK FOR TRENT, CLARK -- IT'LL MAKE US THE LAUGHING STOCK OF ALL THE OTHER PAPERS.
LET 'EM LAUGH! THE LOUDER THEY CACKLE NOW, THE MORE SHEEPISH THEY'LL FEEL LATER!

LARRY TRENT COMES BACK!
BY CLARK KENT
IN A SURPRISING BATTLE TONIGHT LARRY TRENT, EX-HEAVYWEIGHT CHAMPION OF THE WORLD, WRESTED THE DECISION FROM THE FAVORITE 'SLUGGER' BARNES.
TO SAY THAT FIGHT FANS WERE AMAZED
THE WINNER
1939 McClure Newspaper Syndicate
AS THE MONTHS PASS --
MILWAUKEE JOURNAL
TRENT WINS TENTH STRAIGHT VICTORY
SCORE TECHNICAL KNOCKOUT IN 1ST.
BY PAUL CASSIDY
SPORTS
BOSTON TRANSCRIPT
LARRY KAYOES RIVAL; TITLE BATTLE NEXT
50.
CHAMPIONSHIP MATCH TOMORROW NIGHT
MILLION DOLLAR GATE EXPECTED
FISTICUFF FOLLOWERS WILL BE FLOCKING TO THE ARENA IN DROVES TOMORROW TO WITNESS THE BATTLE OF THE CENTURY. THE PRESENT TITLE-HOLDER, FRANKIE MASTERS, CLAIMS HE WILL SEND THE CHALLEN LARRY TRENT, BACK INTO OBSCURI MANY, HOWEVER, BELIEVE

THE DAY BEFORE THE BIG FIGHT...
DO YOU MIND IF WE DON'T SPAR TODAY? --I...I'M FEELING LOW!
AW C'MON, LARRY! PUT UP THOSE DUKES! THAT'S NO WAY FOR TH' NEXT HEAVYWEIGHT CHAMP OF THE WORLD TO TALK!
I'VE BEEN THINKIN'! -- S'POSE YOU DO WIN TH' TITLE UNDER MY NAME, THEN ALLOW ME TO TAKE TH' CREDIT. -- WHAT DOES THAT GIVE ME BUT A HOLLOW VICTORY!
SO THAT'S WHAT'S BOTHERING YOU! LISTEN, OUR CONSTANT TRAINING HAS PUT YOU IN EXCELLENT CONDITION... TOMORROW, YOU'RE GOING TO ENTER THE RING AND WIN THAT TITLE!
ME!
1939, McClure Newspaper Syndicate
YA-HOO! I'LL KNOCK 'IM SILLY!
ATTABOY!
51
LATER --
THE OTHER NEWSPAPERS HAVE BEEN KIDDING US BECAUSE OF YOUR PLUGGING TRENT FOR THE TITLE -- ARE YOU SURE HE'S GOING TO WIN?
SO POSITIVE THAT I'VE WRITTEN THE FIGHT'S OUTCOME IN ADVANCE! HERE IT IS, READY FOR PRINT!

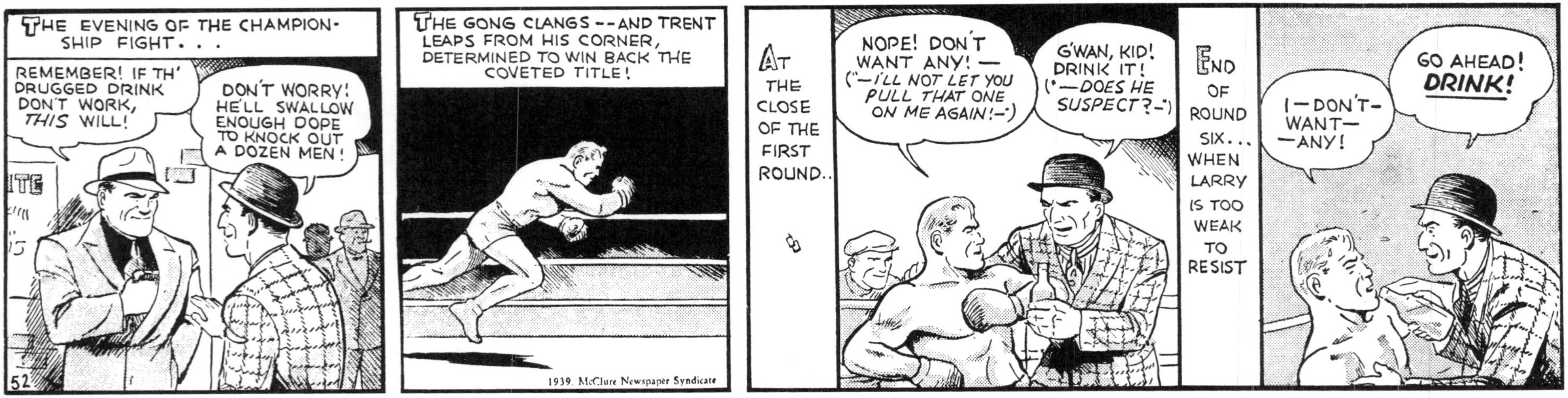
THE EVENING OF THE CHAMPIONSHIP FIGHT...
REMEMBER! IF TH' DRUGGED DRINK DON'T WORK, THIS WILL!
DON'T WORRY! HE'LL SWALLOW ENOUGH DOPE TO KNOCK OUT A DOZEN MEN!
52
THE GONG CLANGS -- AND TRENT LEAPS FROM HIS CORNER, DETERMINED TO WIN BACK THE COVETED TITLE!
1939, McClure Newspaper Syndicate
AT THE CLOSE OF THE FIRST ROUND..
NOPE! DON'T WANT ANY! -- ("--I'LL NOT LET YOU PULL THAT ONE ON ME AGAIN!--")
G'WAN, KID! DRINK IT! ("--DOES HE SUSPECT?--")
END OF ROUND SIX... WHEN LARRY IS TOO WEAK TO RESIST
I--DON'T-WANT--ANY!
GO AHEAD! DRINK!

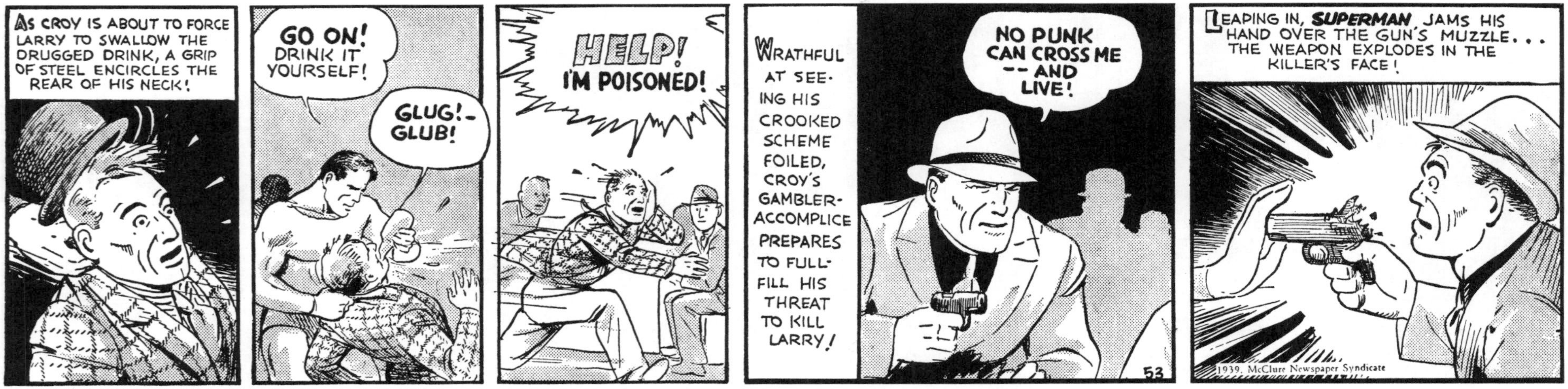
AS CROY IS ABOUT TO FORCE LARRY TO SWALLOW THE DRUGGED DRINK, A GRIP OF STEEL ENCIRCLES THE REAR OF HIS NECK!
GO ON! DRINK IT YOURSELF!
GLUG!-GLUB!
HELP! I'M POISONED!
WRATHFUL AT SEEING HIS CROOKED SCHEME FOILED, CROY'S GAMBLER-ACCOMPLICE PREPARES TO FULL-FILL HIS THREAT TO KILL LARRY!
NO PUNK CAN CROSS ME -- AND LIVE!
53
LEAPING IN, SUPERMAN JAMS HIS HAND OVER THE GUN'S MUZZLE... THE WEAPON EXPLODES IN THE KILLER'S FACE!
1939, McClure Newspaper Syndicate

UNAWARE OF THE DRAMA ENACTED OUTSIDE THE RING, LARRY KNOCKS DOWN HIS OPPONENT FOR THE COUNT!
THE WINNER -- AND NEW HEAVY-WEIGHT CHAMPION OF THE WORLD!
LATER — AS LARRY GOES TO THANK THE MAN REALLY RE-SPONSIBLE FOR HIS COMEBACK
THAT'S STRANGE! THE APARTMENT'S EMPTY...EXCEPT FOR THIS NOTE!
54
You don't need me any longer, Larry, and so -- farewell
Sincere con-gratulations!
SUPERMAN
1939, McClure Newspaper Syndicate
WHAT BEATS ME, CLARK, IS HOW THIS STORY YOU WROTE IN ADVANCE OF THE FIGHT, SCOOPING THE OTHER PAPERS, COULD HAVE PREDICTED THE OUTCOME IN SUCH DETAIL!
JUST FORE-SIGHT, CHIEF! -- MERELY FORESIGHT!
Beginning MONDAY
A THRILLING NEW ADVENTURE STARRING
SUPERMAN
THE MAN OF TOMORROW
!

EPISODE FOUR
JEWEL SMUGGLERS

THE EDITOR'S WAITING TO SEE YOU IN HIS OFFICE, KENT. BETTER HURRY!
BE RIGHT WITH HIM!
55
I WON'T STAND FOR IT! YOU CAN'T DO THIS TO ME!
I'M SORRY, LOIS, BUT IT'S BACK TO THE LOVELORN COLUMN FOR YOU. IT'S SAFER, ANYWAY!
WANT ME, CHIEF?
1939, McClure Newspaper Syndicate
CLARK, YOU COVERED TRENT'S COMEBACK SO WELL, I'M PROMOTING YOU!
GEE... THAT'S *SWELL*!
FOR *YOU*!
OH, HOW I HATE CLARK KENT! — I TELL YOU, HE DELIBERATELY SET OUT TO TAKE MY JOB FROM ME!
SH-H-H! — HERE HE COMES NOW!

ABOUT YOUR BEING DEMOTED, LOIS -- PLEASE BELIEVE ME WHEN I SAY I'M SORRY!
I'M FAR FROM BEING HAPPY ABOUT IT MYSELF!
56
LET ME TAKE YOU TO SOME GAY PLACE TONIGHT... I'M VERY EXPERT AT CONSOLING PEOPLE
SORRY... -- NOT INTERESTED
YOU DIDN'T HAVE TO TURN HIM DOWN *THAT* COLDLY!
THE LESS I SEE OF THAT WORM THE BETTER!
1939, McClure Newspaper Syndicate
MAY I SEE THE LOVELORN EDITOR!
I'LL TELL HER YOU'RE HERE!

I—I'M DESPERATE! I'VE COME TO YOU AS A LAST RESORT!
TELL ME YOUR TROUBLES — IF I CAN OFFER HELPFUL ADVICE, I'LL BE GLAD TO DO SO!
IT'S ABOUT MY HUSBAND: LEW FRAWLEY. WE GOT ALONG FINE 'TILL HE TOOK TO HANGING OUT WITH A TOUGH BUNCH AT JOE'S JOINT!
57
NOW HE RARELY COMES HOME. . . WHEN HE DOES, HE BEATS ME! — — THIS IS A PHOTO OF HIM.
1939, McClure Newspaper Syndicate
AND WORSE -- I THINK HE'S JOINED A GANG OF **SMUGGLERS**!
GIVE ME A FEW DAYS.— PERHAPS I'LL BE ABLE TO HELP YOU GET YOUR HUSBAND BACK. — — ("— GOLLY! THIS SOUNDS LIKE THE TIP TO A GREAT STORY THAT MAY WIN ME BACK MY NEWS REPORTER JOB!—")

BR-RR! — DID LOIS TURN ME DOWN COLD WHEN I ASKED FOR THAT DATE!
58
I'VE CHANGED MY MIND, CLARK. I'D BE *DELIGHTED* TO ACCOMPANY YOU TONIGHT!
YOU **WHAT-?** G-GOSH! -- THAT'S GREAT!
1939, McClure Newspaper Syndicate
THAT EVENING
MIND IF I INSTRUCT THE CAB DRIVER WHERE TO GO?
NOT AT ALL!
JOE'S JOINT! —WHY THIS IS ONE OF THE TOUGHEST JOINTS ON THE WATERFRONT!
I KNOW IT! S'MATTER? AFRAID TO ENTER?
JOE'S JOINT

IT WAS STUBBORN AND DANGEROUS FOR YOU TO INSIST WE COME HERE!
NOT SCARED, ARE YOU? — A LITTLE SLUMMING WILL DO YOU GOOD!
("—THE MAN AT THAT TABLE... HE'S LEW FRAWLEY! —I'VE GOT TO CATCH HIS ATTENTION!—")
59
DELIBERATELY, LOIS WINKS...!
1939, McClure Newspaper Syndicate
UM-MM! — IS THAT GOOD-LOOKER GIVIN' YOU TH' EYE!
WATCH ME GIVE 'ER A BREAK AN' CUT IN!
GO TO IT, LEW!

HI-YA, BABE! — HOW'S ABOUT YOU AN' ME DANCIN'?
HOLD ON! THIS ISN'T A "CUT-IN" DANCE!
DON'T GET FLIP WID ME! —BEAT IT, PUNK!
ULP-!
1939, McClure Newspaper Syndicate 60
AS LEW DANCES OFF WITH LOIS, CLARK TURNS PALE AND TREMBLES WITH HELPLESS RAGE... IN KEEPING WITH HIS ASSUMED ATTITUDE OF COWARDLINESS
YOU'RE SO MANLY... AND STRONG!
WANTA FEEL MY MUSCLE?
WHILE LOIS CLEVERLY INFLATES FRAWLEY'S EGO, SHE SLIPS A FOLDED PAPER FROM HIS POCKET!

LATER -- WITHIN THE PRIVACY OF THE LADIES' ROOM, LOIS SCANS THE PAPER SHE HAD TAKEN FROM FRAWLEY
WHAT A BREAK!
Jewel shipment coming in this evening Barney
SAY! — IS THAT DAME *WILD* ABOUT ME!
YA DUMB SAP! WE SAW HER SWIPE A NOTE RIGHT OUTA YER POCKET.
YA'VE BEEN PLAYED FER A SUCKER! GONNA LET HER GET AWAY WITH IT?
1939, McClure Newspaper Syndicate
BUT LOIS —!
I'M LEAVING! — I WON'T STAY HERE ANOTHER SECOND WITH A COWARDLY WEAKLING WHO ALLOWS A GIRL TO BE INSULTED!
KEEP WALKIN'
AN' NOT A PEEP OUTA EITHER OF YA!

GO ON! GET IN!
C'MON! SPILL IT! — YER A DETECTIVE AREN'T YA?
YOU'RE HURTING ME!
L-LET HER ALONE!
I WARNED YA T'KEEP THAT MOUTH *SHUT!*
62
HELP!
HE'LL DROWN! HE CAN'T SWIM!
WHO CARES!
1939, McClure Newspaper Syndicate

LEAVE ME TO DROWN, WILL THEY? — WELL, THEY'VE GOT ANOTHER GUESS COMING!
KENT SWIMS UNDERWATER AT TERRIFIC SPEED...
1939, McClure Newspaper Syndicate 63
I BEAT THE BOAT TO THE WHARF. — HERE IT COMES, NOW!
THE THUGS DRAG LOIS INTO A SHACK ON THE WHARF, COMPLETELY UN-AWARE THEY ARE BEING OBSERVED BY A FANTASTIC, CLOAKED FIGURE...

TALK!
PLEASE BELIEVE ME! I'M NOT A DETECTIVE. — JUST A REPORTER IN SEARCH OF A STORY!
64
1939, McClure Newspaper Syndicate
THEN HERE'S YER STORY! SEE THESE JEWELS? WE SMUGGLED 'EM IN FROM EUROPE FOR PEOPLE WHO WANT T'ESCAPE PAYIN' CUSTOM DUTIES!
BUT WHY TELL ME THIS?
BECAUSE YOU'LL NEVER LIVE T'PRINT IT!
DON'T SHOOT-- IF YOU VALUE YOUR OWN SKIN!
WHAT--? WHO IN--?
TOO LATE! — LEW'S FINGER CONTRACTS -- A DEAFENING EXPLOSION...AND A DEADLY LEADEN MISSILE IS LAUNCHED AT THE HELPLESS GIRL REPORTER!
CROSS YOUR FINGERS, FOLKS!

SIMULTANEOUS WITH THE EXPLOSION, SUPERMAN SPRINTS PARALLEL WITH THE BULLET IN THE STRANGEST RACE THE WORLD HAS EVER SEEN!
1939, McClure Newspaper Syndicate
BULL'SEYE!
A FRACTION OF A SECOND BEFORE IT CAN STRIKE LOIS, SUPERMAN SPRINGS BEFORE HER AND PERMITS THE BULLET TO BOUNCE OFF HIS SUPER-TOUGH SKIN!
AND NOW FOR YOU GENTS..!
SHORTLY AFTER, HIGH ABOVE THE CITY --

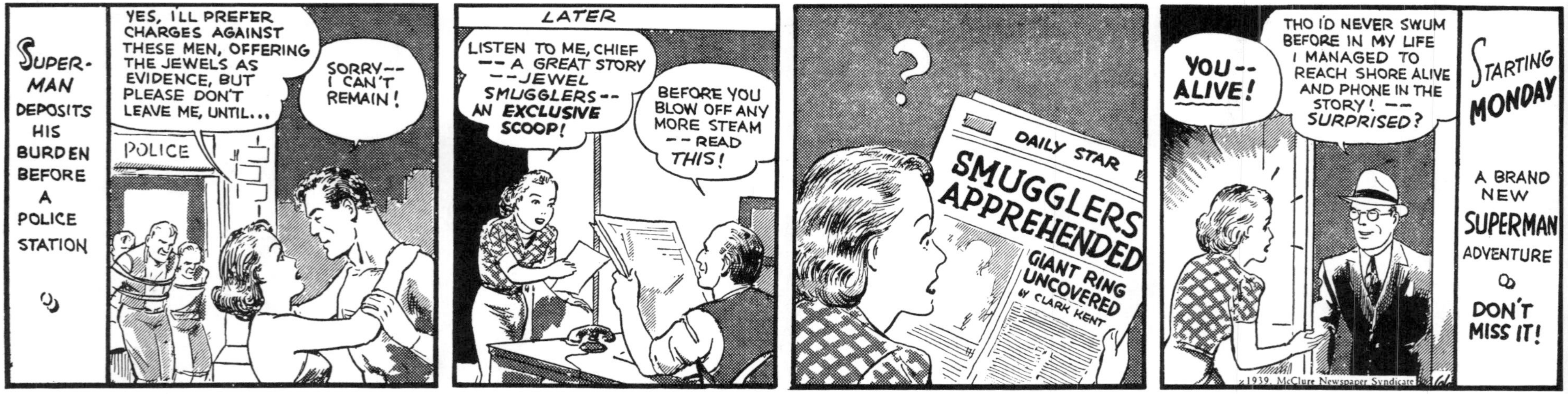
SUPER-MAN DEPOSITS HIS BURDEN BEFORE A POLICE STATION
YES, I'LL PREFER CHARGES AGAINST THESE MEN, OFFERING THE JEWELS AS EVIDENCE, BUT PLEASE DON'T LEAVE ME, UNTIL...
SORRY-- I CAN'T REMAIN!
POLICE
LATER
LISTEN TO ME, CHIEF -- A GREAT STORY --JEWEL SMUGGLERS-- AN EXCLUSIVE SCOOP!
BEFORE YOU BLOW OFF ANY MORE STEAM -- READ THIS!
?
DAILY STAR
SMUGGLERS APPREHENDED
GIANT RING UNCOVERED
BY CLARK KENT
YOU-- ALIVE!
THO I'D NEVER SWUM BEFORE IN MY LIFE I MANAGED TO REACH SHORE ALIVE AND PHONE IN THE STORY! -- SURPRISED?
1939, McClure Newspaper Syndicate
STARTING MONDAY
A BRAND NEW SUPERMAN ADVENTURE
DON'T MISS IT!

EPISODE FIVE
SKYSCRAPER OF DEATH

Superman—By Jerry Siegel and Joe Shuster *What's Wrong?* (Copyright, 1939.)

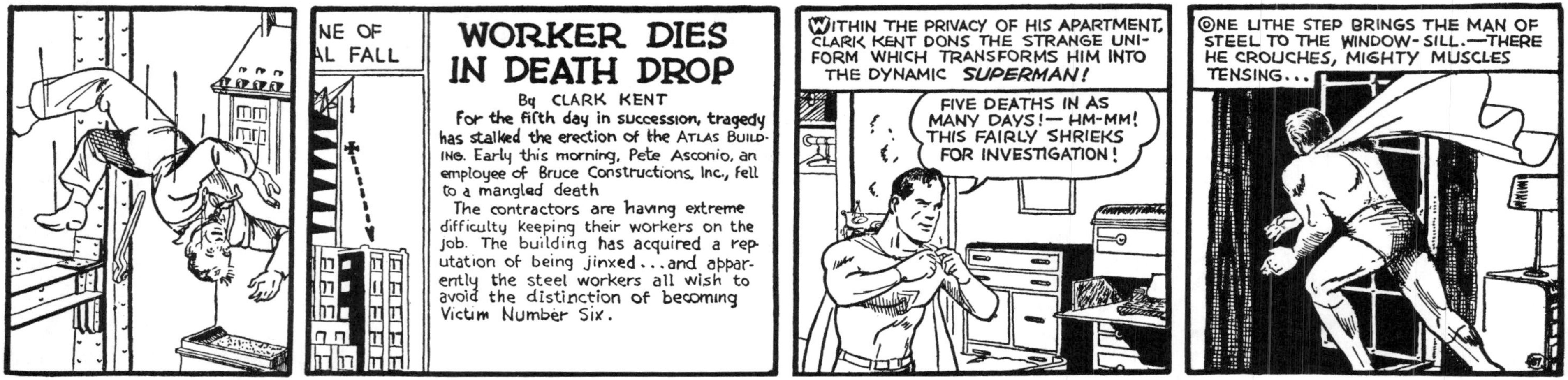
NE OF
AL FALL
WORKER DIES IN DEATH DROP
By CLARK KENT
For the fifth day in succession, tragedy has stalked the erection of the ATLAS BUILDING. Early this morning, Pete Asconio, an employee of Bruce Constructions, Inc., fell to a mangled death
The contractors are having extreme difficulty keeping their workers on the job. The building has acquired a reputation of being jinxed ... and apparently the steel workers all wish to avoid the distinction of becoming Victim Number Six.
WITHIN THE PRIVACY OF HIS APARTMENT, CLARK KENT DONS THE STRANGE UNIFORM WHICH TRANSFORMS HIM INTO THE DYNAMIC SUPERMAN!
FIVE DEATHS IN AS MANY DAYS!— HM-MM! THIS FAIRLY SHRIEKS FOR INVESTIGATION!
ONE LITHE STEP BRINGS THE MAN OF STEEL TO THE WINDOW-SILL.—THERE HE CROUCHES, MIGHTY MUSCLES TENSING...

Superman—By Jerry Siegel and Joe Shuster *Superman Investigates* (Copyright, 1939.)

SUPERMAN'S STEELY MUSCLES LAUNCH HIM OUT INTO THE NIGHT!
AH -- THERE IT IS!
..... A FEW MOMENTS LATER THE FANTASTIC, CLOAKED FIGURE HURTLES DOWN UPON THE GIRDERS ATOP THE SKYSCRAPER OF MYSTERY!

Superman—By Jerry Siegel and Joe Shuster *A Clear Coast* (Copyright, 1939.)

SILHOUETTED BY THE SILVERY MOONLIGHT AGAINST THE SKYSCRAPER'S MASSIVE BLACK SHADOWS, SUPERMAN COMMENCES TO EXAMINE THE STRUCTURE, WHEN...
WHAT'S THAT?
...HIS SUPER-HEARING DETECTS THE SOUND OF THE RISING ELEVATOR!
69.
SOMEONE'S COMING!
THE ELEVATOR CLANKS TO A STOP. OUT SHUFFLES... THE NIGHT WATCHMAN!
THE COAST IS CLEAR!

Superman—By Jerry Siegel and Joe Shuster *Dirty Work* (Copyright, 1939.)

OUT ONTO A GIRDER EDGES THE NIGHT WATCHMAN
70
NOW TO GET TO WORK!
STEADILY HE SAWS UNTIL THE GIRDER IS CUT ALMOST COMPLETELY THRU...
TOMORROW THERE'LL BE ANOTHER FATAL ACCIDENT. —HOW UNFORTUNATE!
BUT AS HE COMMENCES TO RETURN ALONG THE STEEL GIRDER...
WHAT IN—? HOW DID YOU GET HERE!

Superman—By Jerry Siegel and Joe Shuster *A Strange Apparition* (Copyright, 1939.)

WHO ARE YOU ? —WHY DON'T YOU ANSWER ME?
YOU'RE A DETECTIVE THAT'S WHO YOU ARE!.
WORDLESSLY, SUPERMAN ADVANCES
STAND BACK! —ANOTHER STEP FORWARD, AND I SHOOT!
DESPERATELY, THE TERRIFIED WATCH-MAN EMPTIES HIS REVOLVER AT THE FANTASTIC FIGURE . . . !
I WARNED YA!

Superman—By Jerry Siegel and Joe Shuster *Another Accident.* (Copyright, 1939.)

IN THE FACE OF A HAIL OF BULLETS, SUPERMAN CONTINUES ON...ON...
DIE! DIE!—I'VE SHOT YOU! WHY DON'T YOU FALL DEAD?
HYSTERICALLY, THE NIGHT WATCHMAN RETREATS...THEN
DOWN TOWARD THE DISTANT STREET HURTLES THE WATCHMAN, A VICTIM OF HIS OWN FIENDISH DEVICE...!

uperman—By Jerry Siegel and Joe Shuster *Down—Down!* (Copyright, 1939.)

DOWN AFTER THE WATCHMAN'S FIGURE DIVES *SUPERMAN!*
I'VE GOT TO SAVE HIM!
CLOSER TOWARD THE EARTH HURTLE THE TWO BODIES, THE SPACE BETWEEN THEM GRADUALLY NARROWING...
HE'S HAD A HEAD-START! — CAN I REACH HIM?
GOT HIS HEEL!
BRUCE CONST. -INC.-
73
WITH THE GROUND BUT INCHES AWAY HOW CAN *SUPERMAN* SAVE THE WATCHMAN FROM A MANGLED DOOM?

Superman—By Jerry Siegel and Joe Shuster *Made It!* (Copyright, 1939.)

WITH ONLY INSTANTS TO ACT, *SUPERMAN* WHIRLS THE WATCHMAN UP INTO THE AIR ABOVE HIM...
UPSY-DAISY!
WHAM! — *SUPERMAN* STRIKES THE GROUND AMIDST FLYING EARTH.... TREMENDOUS MUSCLES CUSHION THE SHOCK...
...WITH INCREDIBLE AGILITY, THE MAN OF STEEL WHIRLS...
...AND CATCHES THE DESCENDING MAN IN HIS ARMS!
MADE IT!
74.

Superman—By Jerry Siegel and Joe Shuster *Orders From the Gang* (Copyright, 1939.)

WHEN THE WATCHMAN REVIVES...
I'M GOING TO ASK YOU A FEW QUESTIONS.
MY HEART... CAN'T LAST MUCH LONGER!
QUICK! TELL ME WHY YOU KILLED THE STEEL WORKERS!
I WAS ONLY OBEYING ORDERS. I BELONG TO THE GANG OF--OF--
BRUCE CONST -INC.-
OF WHO?
BUTCH GROGAN!
DEAD... HEART-FAILURE! THE EXCITEMENT WAS TOO MUCH FOR HIM!
75

Superman—By Jerry Siegel and Joe Shuster *Impolite!* (Copyright, 1939.)

SO BUTCH GROGAN IS THE MAN RESPONSIBLE FOR THE DEATHS! —BUT WHAT CAN HIS MOTIVE BE?
76.
WHEN GROGAN'S RESIDENCE IS REACHED..
WOTTAYA WANT?
I'VE COME TO SEE BUTCH!
HE AIN'T IN!
DON'T YOU KNOW IT'S IMPOLITE TO SLAM A DOOR IN SOMEONE'S FACE?

Superman—By Jerry Siegel and Joe Shuster *An Insistent Guest* (Copyright, 1939.)

WOTSA IDEA?
I SAID I WANT TO SEE BUTCH! WILL YOU LEAD ME TO HIM OR...!
I TELL YA! HE AIN'T HERE!
I'LL FIND THAT OUT FOR MYSELF!
SUPERMAN SEARCHES THE PLACE...
LEMME GO!
PIPE DOWN!
LATER...
I TOLD YA HE AIN'T IN! YA SATISFIED NOW?
NOPE!—TELL ME WHERE HE'S GONE!
77

Superman—By Jerry Siegel and Joe Shuster *What's the Super-Degree?* (Copyright, 1939.)

HONEST! I DON'T KNOW WHERE BUTCH WENT!
BETTER TALK! I HAVE WAYS OF MAKING PEOPLE LOOSEN THEIR TONGUE!
LEGGO! WHERE YA TAKIN' ME?
OUTSIDE!
THIS IS YOUR LAST CHANCE! GOING TO TELL ME WHERE BUTCH IS?
I-DON'T-KNOW!
YOU'VE HEARD OF THE THIRD-DEGREE.
COMING MONDAY --THE "SUPER-DEGREE"!
78.

Superman—By Jerry Siegel and Joe Shuster *The Super-Degree* (Copyright, 1939.)

SEIZING THE QUAVERING HENCHMAN, SUPERMAN HURLS HIM UPWARD . . .
LET'S PLAY "CATCH"! — YOU BE THE BALL!
UP-UP—SPEEDS THE SHRIEKING HUMAN MISSILE . . . .
YE-EE!
. . . . THEN COMMENCES TO PLUMMET DOWNWARD IN AN AWFUL DROP.
H-H-HELP!
GOING TO TALK OR SHALL I KEEP ON AMUSING MYSELF?
FOR PETE'S SAKE, LEMME ALONE! — — I DON'T KNOW NOTHIN'!

Superman—By Jerry Siegel and Joe Shuster —*See SUPERMAN in Color — Starting in the Post-Dispatch Next Sunday.* (Copyright, 1939.)

SUPERMAN CONTINUES HIS EFFORTS TO MAKE THE STUBBORN HENCHMAN TALK . . . .
BON VOYAGE!
READY TO TALK?
YES, YES! — — IF YOU'LL LEAVE ME ALONE!
TELL ME! WHERE IS HE?
BUTCH WENT TO—
LOOKIN' FER ME?

Superman—By Jerry Siegel and Joe Shuster *Superman is coming in color—Next Sunday in the Post-Dispatch.* (Copyright, 1939.)

WHY'D YA WANT T'SEE ME? SPILL IT!
WILL YOU PLEASE PUT THAT GUN AWAY! —IT ANNOYS ME!
WHY YOU MEASLY PUNK, I'LL BLOW YOUR HEAD OFF!
BUT BEFORE THE GANGSTER CAN PULL THE TRIGGER...OUT DARTS SUPERMAN'S HAND
GIVE ME THAT!
81
--AND CRUSHES BUTCH'S PISTOL INTO A SHAPELESS PULP!

uperman—By Jerry Siegel and Joe Shuster **Superman's Adventures in Color Start Sunday in the Post-Dispatch** (Copyright, 1939.)

TH' GAT! YA CRUSHED IT LIKE IT WAS MADE OUTA PUTTY!
RIGHT! AND IF YOU DON'T TELL ME WHAT I WANT TO KNOW, I'LL GET TO WORK ON YOU!
SEIZING A HEAVY CLUB, BUTCH'S HENCH-MAN STEALS UP ON TIP-TOE TOWARD THE MAN OF TOMORROW'S BACK...
TAKE THAT!
SUPERMAN SCARCELY FEELS THE BLOW ...BUT THE CLUB BOUNCES BACK AND KNOCKS OUT ITS WIELDER!
CR-RACK
82

Superman—By Jerry Siegel and Joe Shuster **SUPERMAN IN COLOR—IN THE POST-DISPATCH SUNDAY.** (Copyright, 1939.)

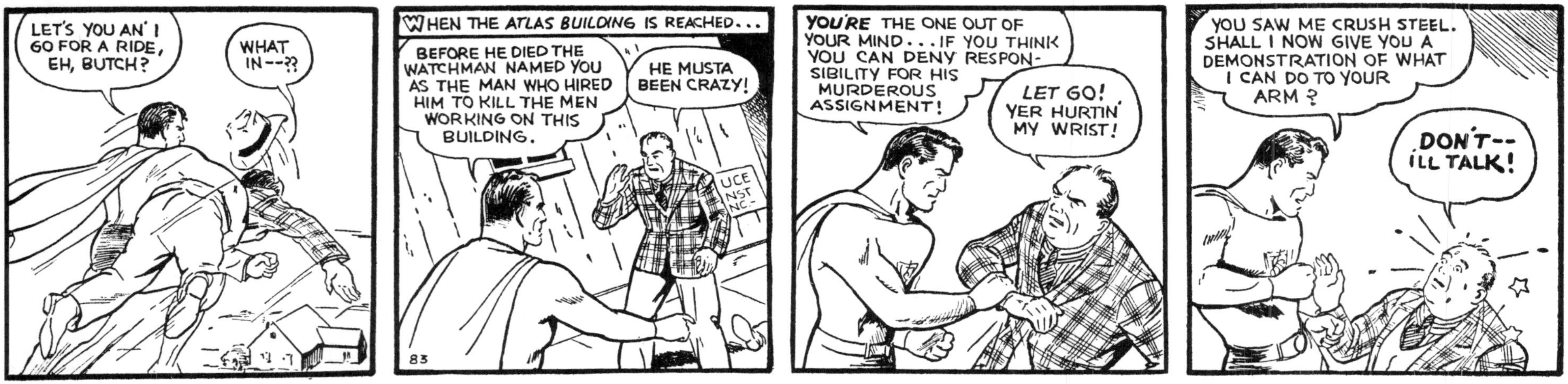
LET'S YOU AN' I GO FOR A RIDE, EH, BUTCH?
WHAT IN--??
WHEN THE ATLAS BUILDING IS REACHED...
BEFORE HE DIED THE WATCHMAN NAMED YOU AS THE MAN WHO HIRED HIM TO KILL THE MEN WORKING ON THIS BUILDING.
HE MUSTA BEEN CRAZY!
83
YOU'RE THE ONE OUT OF YOUR MIND... IF YOU THINK YOU CAN DENY RESPONSIBILITY FOR HIS MURDEROUS ASSIGNMENT!
LET GO! YER HURTIN' MY WRIST!
YOU SAW ME CRUSH STEEL. SHALL I NOW GIVE YOU A DEMONSTRATION OF WHAT I CAN DO TO YOUR ARM?
DON'T-- I'LL TALK!

Superman—By Jerry Siegel and Joe Shuster **Tomorrow's the Big Day! Superman in Color in the Sunday Post-Dispatch.** (Copyright, 1939.)

LET'S HAVE IT!
I WAS HIRED BY NAT GRAYSON, PRESIDENT OF THE AKME CONSTRUCTION COMPANY, TO SLOW UP TH' ERECTION OF THIS BUILDING THRU ANY MEANS!
HE WANTS T' PREVENT BRUCE CONSTRUCTIONS INC. FROM COMPLETING TH' JOB WITHIN TH' TIME REQUIRED IN THEIR CONTRACT!
I SEE!—IF GRAYSON S'UCCEEDS HE'LL DESTROY HIS GREATEST BUSINESS RIVAL AND DOMINATE THE CONSTRUCTION FIELD!
WHAT'S GOING ON HERE? DON'T EITHER OF YOU MOVE!
A COP!
SORRY... GOTTA GO!
STOP IN THE NAME OF THE LAW!
84

Superman—By Jerry Siegel and Joe Shuster

Butch Pays the Penalty

(Copyright, 1939.)

YA GOTTA LEAVE TOWN, GRAYSON! A GUY WITH TH' STRENGTH OF FIFTY ELEPHANTS IS COMIN' T'GET YA!
THANKS FOR THE TIP, BUTCH! I'LL BE PREPARED!
DRU
THOUGHT YOU'D GET AWAY, EH? STOP OR I'LL SHOOT!
BLAST TH' LUCK!
--DISREGARDING THE ORDER TO HALT, BUTCH MAKES A DASH FOR FREEDOM.. AND DIES!
85

Superman—By Jerry Siegel and Joe Shuster

A Warning

(Copyright, 1939.)

SO NAT GRAYSON IS THE SCOUNDREL REALLY RESPONSIBLE FOR THE DEATHS! WELL, HE'LL PAY FOR IT!
86
IT'S A GOOD THING I HAD THIS ROOM OF METAL CONSTRUCTED AS A SAFETY MEASURE. IT'LL COME IN HANDY NOW!
AS SUPERMAN ENTERS THE GRAYSON RESIDENCE A LOUDSPEAKER BLARES A WARNING...
GO AWAY... AT ONCE! HEED THIS WARNING ..OR DIE!

Superman—By Jerry Siegel and Joe Shuster

Can Superman Get Through?

(Copyright, 1939.)

YOU CAN'T POSSIBLY GET AT ME IN THIS METAL ROOM, AND UNLESS YOU LEAVE AT ONCE, I'LL BLAST YOU OUT OF EXISTENCE!
I'VE PLANTED BOMBS AT VARIOUS SPOTS. PHOTO-ELECTRIC CELLS KEEP ME INFORMED AS TO YOUR EXACT POSITION! FOR THE LAST TIME—KEEP BACK!
87
AS THE MAN OF STEEL CONTINUES TO ADVANCE ALONG THE HALL...

Superman—By Jerry Siegel and Joe Shuster

Into the Steel Sanctum

(Copyright, 1939.)

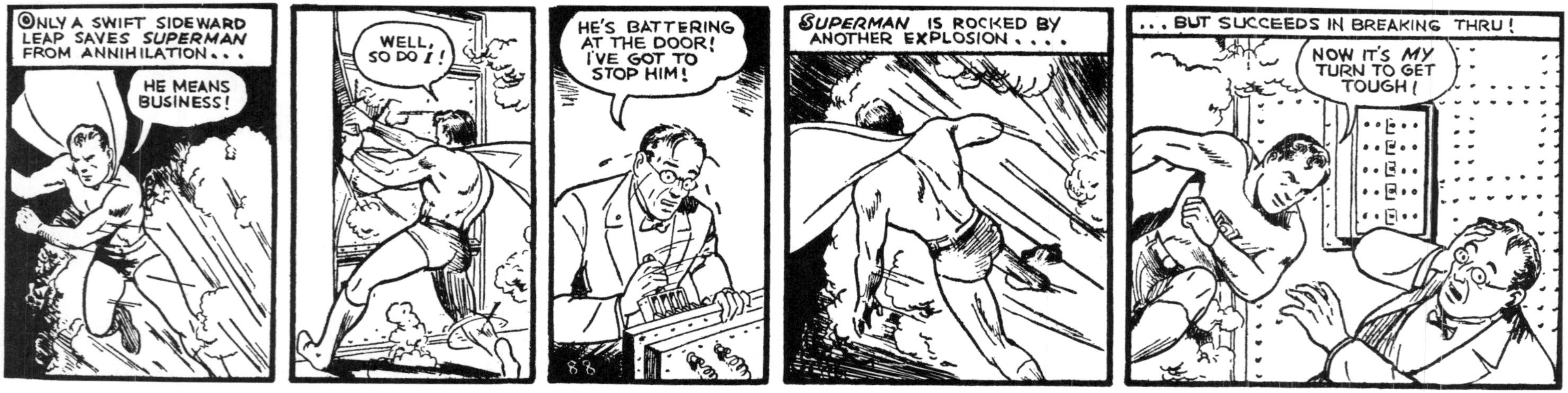

ONLY A SWIFT SIDEWARD LEAP SAVES SUPERMAN FROM ANNIHILATION...
HE MEANS BUSINESS!
WELL, SO DO I!
HE'S BATTERING AT THE DOOR! I'VE GOT TO STOP HIM!
88
SUPERMAN IS ROCKED BY ANOTHER EXPLOSION....
...BUT SUCCEEDS IN BREAKING THRU!
NOW IT'S MY TURN TO GET TOUGH!

Superman—By Jerry Siegel and Joe Shuster *Arrest Me!* (Copyright, 1939.)

PHONE A FULL CONFESSION OF YOUR MURDEROUS *ATLAS BUILDING* OUTRAGES TO THE POLICE, AND I'LL RESIST THE URGE TO WRING YOUR NECK!
DON'T HURT ME!
89
I'M NAT GRAYSON-I'VE A CRIME TO CONFESS -- SEND SOME POLICE OVER AT ONCE!
I'D HOPED I'D HAVE TO USE A LITTLE "PERSUASION" ON YOU!
LISTEN... POLICE SIRENS! THEY'VE COME!
REMEMBER! IF YOU DON'T CONFESS, I'LL COME BACK AND DISH OUT THE JUSTICE YOU DESERVE WITH MY BARE HANDS!
I'M RESPONSIBLE FOR THE DEATH OF THE STEEL WORKERS WHO DIED ON THE *ATLAS BUILDING*. ARREST ME!
FIRST TIME I EVER SAW A GUY SO ANXIOUS TO GET ARRESTED!

Superman—By Jerry Siegel and Joe Shuster *Another Scoop for the Paper* (Copyright, 1939.)

THE DEAD MEN ARE AVENGED...AND SO MY WORK IS DONE!
90.
DAILY STAR
GRAYSON CONVICTED
SENTENCED TO ELECTRIC-CHAIR
by CLARK KENT
YOU HANDLED THE GRAYSON TRIAL BEAUTIFULLY! BUT HOW DID YOU MANAGE TO LEARN OF HIS ARREST BEFORE THE OTHER PAPERS?
JUST LUCK CHIEF! (AND THE ASSISTANCE OF "*SUPERMAN!*")
Starting MONDAY!
ANOTHER THRILLING
SUPERMAN
ADVENTURE

EPISODE SIX
THE MOST DEADLY WEAPON

I'VE A GREAT ASSIGNMENT FOR YOU, CLARK. -- BIG STORY -- PROBABLY MAKE HISTORY!
LET ME AT IT!
PROFESSOR RUNYAN -- A SCIENTIFIC GENIUS. — DASH OVER TO HIS HOME AND SEE WHAT'S UP!
I GOT YOU, CHIEF! BUT WHAT HAS RUNYAN DONE TO MERIT AN INTERVIEW ?
NOTHING MUCH. HE'S JUST SET THE SCIENTIFIC WORLD ON ITS EARS WITH HIS AMAZING INVENTIONS, THAT'S ALL! -- *NOW GET GOING!*
AND I SUPPOSE HE'S GOT SOME NEW DISCOVERY TO ANNOUNCE. -- O.K! I'M ON MY WAY!
LATER
YOU'RE PROFESSOR RUNYON, AREN'T YOU ?
YES! AND YOU MUST BE THE REPORTER FROM THE *DAILY STAR!* -- STEP IN, YOUNG MAN! I'VE A STORY TO TELL THAT SHOULD MAKE YOUR FRONT PAGE!

AND WHAT IS THIS IMPORTANT NEWS YOU WANT TO TELL OUR READERS ?
I, PROFESSOR ADOLPHUS RUNYAN, HAVE DISCOVERED THE MOST DEADLY WEAPON MODERN WARFARE HAS EVER SEEN!
ELUCIDATE, PROFESSOR — ELUCIDATE!
BEHOLD! IN THIS TUBE IS CONTAINED A GAS SO *POWERFUL* THAT IT IS CAPABLE OF PENETRATING ANY TYPE OF GAS-MASK!
1939. McClure Newspaper Syndicate
THOSE ARE BOASTFUL WORDS, PROFESSOR. — CAN YOU *PROVE* THEM ?
I KNEW YOU WOULD BE SKEPTICAL -- SO, I WAS PREPARED. COME WITH ME!
PERMIT ME TO INTRODUCE AMBROSE!
SAY! — WHAT IS THIS! A GAG ?

WHAT HAS AMBROSE TO DO WITH YOUR DISCOVERY?
AMBROSE IS GOING TO ILLUSTRATE THE DEADLY POWER OF MY GAS!
AFTER RUNYAN PLACES THE MONKEY WITHIN A GLASS JAR . . .
THE CHAMBER IS FILLING WITH ORDINARY GAS. AS YOU CAN SEE, AMBROSE IS UNAFFECTED!
BUT NOW I RELEASE MY NEW TYPE OF GAS INTO THE JAR! -- WATCH WHAT HAPPENS . . .
1939. McClure Newspaper Syndicate.
HE'S DEAD!
RIGHT! MY GAS PENETRATED HIS GAS-MASK! — NOW DO YOU BELIEVE ME WHEN I SAY THAT THE WORLD HAS NEVER SEEN A DISCOVERY OF SUCH VAST MILITARY IMPORT?

YOU'VE CERTAINLY GOT SOMETHING THERE, PROFESSOR. WHAT DO YOU INTEND DOING WITH IT?
I'LL TURN IT OVER TO OUR WAR DEPARTMENT -- BUT ONLY IN THE CASE OF A DEFENSIVE WAR!
THINK SO?
BARTOW!
BEAT IT, YOU!
WE WANT TO SEE THE PROFESSOR -- ALONE . .
BUT -- I HAVEN'T FINISHED MY INTERVIEW!
ARE YOU GOING TO SCRAM, OR DO I HAVE TO GET TOUGH?
I -- I'LL GO!
THAT'S BETTER!
HE AIN'T SO DUMB AT THAT!
1939. McClure Newspaper Syndicate
BUT AS HE LEAVES, CLARK PAUSES OUTSIDE THE DOOR TO EAVESDROP WITH HIS SUPER-SENSITIVE EARS . . .
A PROFESSOR WHO HAS INVENTED A TERRIBLY DESTRUCTIVE GAS -- THREE EVIL-LOOKING GENTS -- THE COMBINATION SPELLS TROUBLE!

WHAT CLARK OVERHEARS . . .
WELL -- ARE YOU GOING TO HAND OVER THE FORMULA FOR THE GAS ?
SO THAT YOU CAN SELL IT TO ARMAMENT PROFITEERS ? NOTHING DOING! GET OUT!
YOU'VE TWENTY FOUR HOURS TO TURN THE SECRET FORMULA OVER TO US -- OR ELSE! GET THAT?
CLARK TRAILS THE INTERNATIONAL RACKETEERS' TAXI . . .
1939, McClure Newspaper Syndicate
. . . TO A BUNGALOW BESIDE A PRIVATE FLYING FIELD.
SO THERE'S WHERE THEY HANG OUT! HM-M! I'LL JUST KEEP THAT IN MIND!

AFTER CLARK RETURNS TO THE NEWS-PAPER OFFICE . . .
I'LL DASH OFF THIS WRITE-UP OF RUNYAN, THEN RETURN TO BARTOW AND HIS FRIENDS FOR A LITTLE 'TALK'!
HERE IT IS, CHIEF... THE INTERVIEW WITH PROFESSOR RUNYAN. — SOME STORY.
JUST A MOMENT WHILE I ANSWER THIS CALL!
1939 McClure Newspaper Syndicate
WHAT'S THAT ? SAY IT AGAIN! — WELL, I'LL BE BLOWED!
WHAT IS IT, CHIEF?
RUNYAN'S JUST BEEN FOUND --MURDERED!

RUNYAN -- MURDERED! ...THOSE THREE MEN WHO THREATENED HIM ARE HIS SLAYERS -- NO DOUBT OF IT!
⇦ EDITOR
PROD. MGR. ⇨
1939, McClure Newspaper Syndicate 97
LATER... WITHIN THE PRIVACY OF HIS APARTMENT, CLARK KENT REMOVES CIVILIAN CLOTHES.
..REVEALING HIS SUPERMAN COSTUME BENEATH!
NOW FOR THEIR HIDEOUT!
THOSE MURDERERS ARE SLATED TO RECEIVE A VISIT FROM SUPERMAN ... AND JUSTICE!

DOWN TOWARDS BARTOW'S BUNGALOW HURTLES A FANTASTIC FIGURE...
WITHIN THE BUNGALOW...
WHY'D YOU HAVE TO KILL RUNYAN AFTER WE GAVE HIM 24 HOURS?
AW, I GOT THERE JUST AS HE WAS ABOUT TO BEAT IT!
C'MON! THE CIVIL WAR IN BORAVIA WON'T WAIT!
BORAVIA -- CIVIL WAR -- SO THAT'S THEIR GAME!
SHORTLY AFTER, THE ARMAMENT RACKETEERS TAKE OFF IN THEIR PRIVATE PLANE....
1939, McClure Newspaper Syndicate

WITH ONE LEAP SUPERMAN SPRINGS ATOP THE DEPARTING AIRPLANE . . .
FOR A MOMENT HE SWAYS . . . ALMOST LOSES HIS FOOTING . . .
OOPS!
1939 McClure Newspaper Syndicate
. . . BUT REGAINS HIS BALANCE!
I'LL JUST MAKE MYSELF COMFORTABLE; AND BIDE MY TIME!

FOR HOURS THE INTERNATIONAL ARMAMENT CROOKS' PLANE CONTINUES ITS FLIGHT, WITH THE MAN OF STEEL CLINGING TIRELESSLY ATOP IT. .
1939 McClure Newspaper Syndicate
ARE WE NEAR BORAVIA?
WE'LL REACH IT IN A FEW MOMENTS!
AND THEN, TO CASH IN ON THAT FORMULA!
SEVERAL MINUTES LATER THE AIRPLANE WINGS SWIFTLY OVER BORAVIA, A SMALL COUNTRY EXHAUSTING ITS LIFE BLOOD IN SENSELESS CIVIL WAR . . . !
SUPERMAN ACTS! — TEARING AT THE PLANE'S METAL SIDES, HE RIPS IT OPEN!
IT'S TIME I HAD A LITTLE TALK WITH BARTOW!

WHAT IN--? HOW DID YOU GET HERE?
NEVER MIND! WHAT YOU SHOULD BE CONCERNED WITH IS-- WHAT I'LL DO NOW THAT I'M HERE!
W-WHAT DO YOU WANT OF ME?
FIRST... THE FORMULA!
WHAT FORMULA? I DON'T KNOW WHAT YOU'RE TALKING ABOUT!
DON'T QUIBBLE! CRACKING YOUR HEAD LIKE AN EGG SHELL WILL BE A MESSY JOB, BUT IF YOU INSIST ON BEING STUBBORN...
1939, McClure Newspaper Syndicate

COWED BY THE SUDDEN APPARITION, THE RACKETEERS CRAVENLY CRINGE...
YOU'RE LYING! ONE OF YOU HAS THAT FORMULA, AND IF YOU DON'T HAND IT OVER..!
BARTOW'S GOT IT!
DON'T TOUCH ME! I'LL-I'LL GET IT FOR YOU! TAKE OVER THE CONTROLS!
THAT'S BETTER!
BUT AS BARTOW ADVANCES TOWARD A CABINET, A CRAFTY GLEAM LIGHTS HIS EYES. WHAT DOES HIS EVIL BRAIN PLOT?
1939, McClure Newspaper Syndicate

SUDDENLY BARTOW WHIRLS, BLAZING AWAY WITH HIS AUTOMATIC, WRECKING THE PLANE'S CONTROLS.
SUCKER!
...THEN LAUNCHES HIMSELF OUT INTO SPACE.
HO! HO! TRICKING HIM WAS A CINCH!
1939, McClure Newspaper Syndicate
SO HE THINKS I'M DONE FOR, EH? WHAT A SURPRISE HE'S DUE FOR!

A CLOAKED FIGURE HURLS ITSELF OUT FROM THE WRECKED PLANE...
...DOWN IT SPEEDS IN A BREATHTAKING PLUNGE..
1939, McClure Newspaper Syndicate
REMEMBER ME?
HUH!
NOW BEHAVE -- OR I'LL TEAR THE PARACHUTE TO SHREDS, AND WOULDN'T THAT BE TOO BAD... FOR YOU!

WITHIN THE ARMAMENT RACKETEERS' CRIPPLED PLANE . . .
WE'RE GOING TO CRASH!
QUICK! —THE PASSENGERS MAY STILL BE ALIVE!
IT'S BARTOW'S PLANE!
1939, McClure Newspaper Syndicate
LUCKY FOR YOU WE CAME ALONG WHEN WE DID! WHERE'S BARTOW?
HE BAILED OUT-- MAY BE IN DANGER-- WE'VE GOT TO FIND HIM!
I SAW A PARACHUTE DESCENDING NEAR THAT HILL!
AS SUPERMAN AND HIS CAPTIVE ALIGHT...
ARE YOU READY TO GIVE ME THAT FORMULA?
HERE IT IS! BUT WHEN LUBANE, THE MUNITIONS MAGNATE, LEARNS I'VE FUMBLED, MY LIFE WILL BE FORFEIT!

WHEN THE SEARCHING PARTY COMES WITHIN VIEW...
GIVE IT BACK! I'VE CHANGED MY MIND!
I WARN YOU, IF...!
STRANGE! I COULD HAVE SWORN I HIT THE GUY WITH THE CAPE!
CAREFUL YOU DON'T HIT BARTOW!
WANTA PLAY, EH? — COME ON!

AS THE SOLDIERS RAM THEIR BAYONETS AGAINST SUPERMAN'S SUPER-TOUGH SKIN, THEY ARE ASTOUNDED AT WHAT FOLLOWS
G-GOOD GOSH! -- LOOK!
THE BAYONET'S BROKEN!
AT THAT MOMENT--A REBEL PLANE STREAKS DOWNWARD AND RELEASES A DEADLY BOMB TOWARD THE STRUGGLING MEN!
1939 McClure Newspaper Syndicate

HE'S STILL ALIVE!
GIVE ME A HAND WITH HIM!
WHEN THE MAN OF STEEL'S BEARERS REACH THEIR CAMP . . .
WE'VE CAPTURED A REBEL, SIR. WHAT ARE YOUR ORDERS?
HEADQUARTERS DEMANDS WE PROMPTLY EXECUTE ALL PRISONERS!
1939. McClure
AND SO IT OCCURS THAT WHEN SUPERMAN REVIVES LATER, IT IS TO FIND HIMSELF FACED BY A FIRING SQUAD.

YOU DON'T LOOK SO VERY DANGEROUS NOW, UP AGAINST THAT WALL! HAVE YOU ANY LAST WORDS?
YES.— WHAT ARE YOU GOING TO DO WITH THE FORMULA?
TURN IT OVER TO LUBANE, THE MUNITIONS MANUFACTURER! — FAREWELL! I LEAVE YOU NOW TO THE CAPTAIN, AND YOUR FATE!
AFTER BARTOW AND HIS TWO HENCHMEN DEPART
© 1939, McClure Newspaper Syndicate
READY-- AIM--!
FIRE!
109.

SUPERMAN GOES DOWN BEFORE A FIRING-SQUAD BARRAGE!
AS THE SQUAD COMMENCES TO MARCH AWAY...
JUST A MINUTE, BOYS!
© 1939, McClure Newspaper Syndicate
TRY AGAIN!
?

I CAN'T UNDERSTAND HOW ALL OF YOU MISSED HIM -- BUT ONE THING I'M SURE OF: *IT WON'T HAPPEN AGAIN!*
HO-HUM! THIS IS BEGINNING TO BORE ME!
OUR GUNS MUST BE FILLED WITH BLANKS! —**OUCH**! MY FOOT!
© 1939, McClure Newspaper Syndicate
SORRY, I HAVEN'T TIME TO STAND AROUND WHILE YOU WASTE AMMUNITION ON ME!

ALONG THE ROAD RACES *SUPERMAN* AT A TERRIFIC RATE, SHELLS EXPLODING ABOUT HIM ON ALL SIDES!
SOON AFTER...
A TOWN—UNDER BOMBARDMENT—HELPLESS WOMEN AND CHILDREN BEING KILLED! I'VE GOT TO HELP THEM!
SUPERMAN DASHES TOWARD THE LONG-RANGE CANNON RESPONSIBLE FOR THE HAVOC--
--AND SMASHES IT!
© 1939, McClure Newspaper Syndicate

SEIZING AN ARMFUL OF AIRCRAFT BOMBS, SUPERMAN LEAPS OFF...!
ANTI-AIRCRAFT GUNS ATTEMPT DESPERATELY TO BLAST THE FANTASTIC FIGURE OUT OF THE SKY!
GET HIM! -- HE'S HEADED TOWARD THE MUNITIONS WORKS!
© 1939, McClure Newspaper Syndicate
THIS'LL BE A SQUARE HIT!
AS SUPERMAN'S BOMBS STRIKE EARTH-THE GREAT MUNITIONS WORKS IS DESTROYED AMIDST TERRIFIC CARNAGE!

A DIRIGIBLE SWERVES TOWARD SUPERMAN DETERMINED TO BLOT HIM OUT BEFORE HE CAN CONTINUE WITH FURTHER DESTRUCTION.
© 1939, McClure Newspaper Syndicate
A FANTASTIC BATTLE WAGES HIGH ABOVE THE EARTH...THE MAN OF TOMORROW SCRAMBLES ATOP THE SKY-VESSEL...
AS SUPERMAN TEARS THE GREAT BALLOON APART, IT FALLS TO ITS DOOM!

MEANWHILE -- A FEW MINUTES PREVIOUS TO SUPERMAN'S AIR-RAID . . .
BARTOW! — YOU'RE SOONER THAN I EXPECTED!
YES, LUBANE! AND WE'VE HAD SEVERAL HAIR-RAISING EXPERIENCES!
NEVER MIND ABOUT THAT! IF YOU'VE GOT THE FORMULA, GIVE IT TO ME!
HERE IT IS! — WE WERE FORCED TO USE -- ER -- DRASTIC METHODS TO SECURE IT!
TAKE THIS FORMULA TO THE LABORATORY AND HURRY IT BACK WITH A SAMPLE OF THE GAS!
YES, SIR!
AFTER THE ASSISTANT DEPARTS -- ABRUPTLY -- THE ROOM IS ROCKED BY A SERIES OF EXPLOSIONS!
WH-WHAT'S THAT?
WE'RE BEING BOMBED!
© 1939, McClure Newspaper Syndicate

THOSE EXPLOSIONS! WHAT'S HAPPENING -- WHAT DO THEY MEAN?
A MAN -- LEAPING THRU THE SKY -- DROPPING BOMBS? YOU MUST BE MAD!
GOOD GRIEF! SUPERMAN — STILL ALIVE!
HE MUST HAVE ESCAPED FROM THE FIRING SQUAD!
© 1939, McClure Newspaper Syndicate
SUPERMAN? WHO'S THAT?
OUR NEMESIS -- A MAN POSSESSING TERRIFIC STRENGTH. HE'S AFTER THE FORMULA!
HERE'S THE GAS AND FORMULA AS YOU REQUESTED.
SUPERMAN, EH? WELL, WHOEVER HE IS, HE CAN'T FRIGHTEN ME! AS LONG AS I HAVE THIS GAS, I NEED FEAR NO ONE!

LATER--AS HE DROPS DOWN ALONG THE SIDE OF THE MUNITIONS ADMINISTRATION BUILDING, SUPERMAN CATCHES HOLD OF A WINDOW...
WITHIN LUBANE'S OFFICE...
YOU'VE GOT THE FORMULA -- NOW GIVE US OUR DOUGH!
WE'RE CLEARING OUT!
TAKE IT-- AND GO!
WE'RE GRABBING THE FIRST PLANE OUT OF HERE THAT WE CAN GET! AND IF YOU'RE WISE, YOU'LL DO THE SAME.
STILL REFERRING TO A MYTHICAL SUPERMAN, EH? SUPERSTITIOUS FOOLS!
© 1939, McClure Newspaper Syndicate
I THINK I'LL GIVE LUBANE A LITTLE TASTE OF SUPERSTITIOUS FEAR!

I'VE GOT IT AT LAST-- WHAT I'VE ALWAYS SOUGHT-- THE MOST HORRIBLY DESTRUCTIVE GAS ON EARTH! NOTHING CAN STOP ME NOW -- NOTHING!
WHO ARE YOU? WHAT DO YOU WANT OF ME?
I'M GOING TO GIVE YOU THE FATE YOU DESERVE, LUBANE, FOR PROMOTING THIS WAR AND PROFITEERING UPON THE DEATH AND MISERY OF OTHERS!
BACK! THIS GLASS VIAL CONTAINS A PORTION OF RUNYAN'S TERRIBLE GAS! ANOTHER STEP FORWARD, AND I'LL SMASH IT!
YOU'RE BLUFFING! --GIVE IT TO ME!
SUPERMAN ADVANCES -- IN HIS EXCITEMENT, LUBANE DROPS THE TUBE... IT SMASHES... DEADLY FUMES ARISE!
YOU FOOL! SEE WHAT YOU'VE DONE? WE'LL BOTH DIE --HORRIBLY!
© 1939, McClure Newspaper Syndicate

HELP ME!...THE PAIN...I-I'M CHOK-ING.. I CAN'T BREATHE!
YOU'RE ONLY GETTING A TASTE OF THE FATE YOU PLANNED TO DOOM OTHERS TO!
DON'T JUST STAND THERE! BLAST YOU! —WHY DON'T YOU DIE?
THE GAS DOESN'T AFFECT MY PHYSICAL STRUCTURE!
ONE LESS VULTURE! HE WON'T NEED THIS FORMULA ANY LONGER!
© 1939, McClure Newspaper Syndicate
AND NOW— FOR THE TOUGHEST TASK OF ALL!

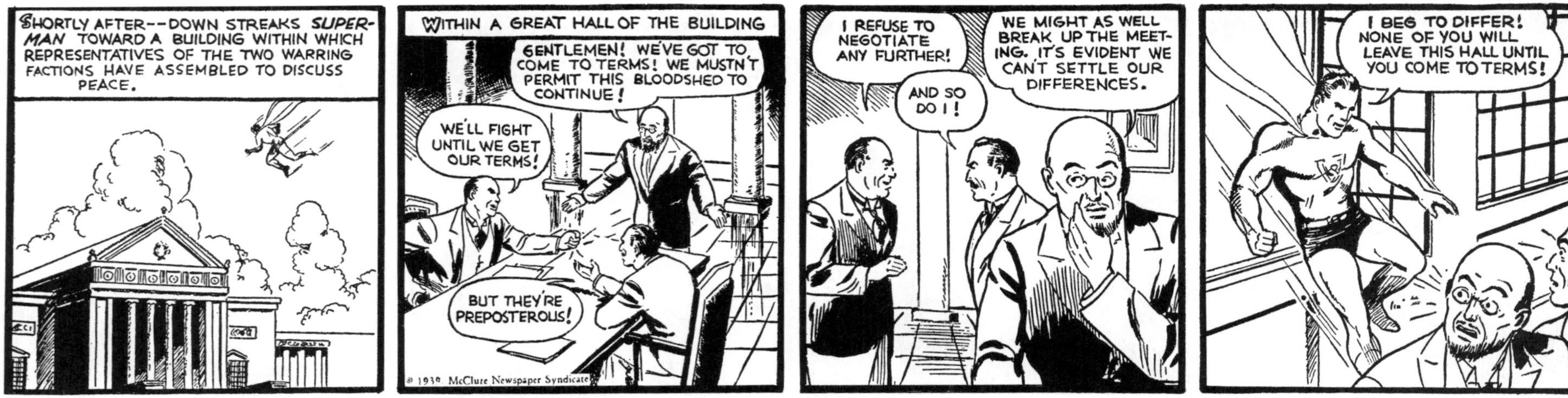
SHORTLY AFTER--DOWN STREAKS SUPERMAN TOWARD A BUILDING WITHIN WHICH REPRESENTATIVES OF THE TWO WARRING FACTIONS HAVE ASSEMBLED TO DISCUSS PEACE.
WITHIN A GREAT HALL OF THE BUILDING
GENTLEMEN! WE'VE GOT TO COME TO TERMS! WE MUSTN'T PERMIT THIS BLOODSHED TO CONTINUE!
WE'LL FIGHT UNTIL WE GET OUR TERMS!
BUT THEY'RE PREPOSTEROUS!
© 1939, McClure Newspaper Syndicate
I REFUSE TO NEGOTIATE ANY FURTHER!
AND SO DO I!
WE MIGHT AS WELL BREAK UP THE MEETING. IT'S EVIDENT WE CAN'T SETTLE OUR DIFFERENCES.
I BEG TO DIFFER! NONE OF YOU WILL LEAVE THIS HALL UNTIL YOU COME TO TERMS!

HOW DARE YOU BREAK IN HERE? GET OUT!
SO YOU NEED A LITTLE PERSUASION, EH?
SEIZING ONE OF THE FOUR PILLARS WHICH SUPPORT THE WALLS, SUPERMAN TEARS AT IT...
A GUY NAMED SAMSON ONCE HAD THE SAME IDEA!
AS SUPERMAN TEARS AT THE PILLAR, FRAGMENTS OF THE CEILING RAIN DOWN ABOUT THE AGHAST MEN!
STOP IT!
YOU—YOU'LL KILL US ALL!
I THOUGHT YOU'D UNDERSTAND THIS BETTER THAN MERE WORDS!
1939, McClure Newspaper Syndicate

DEMOLISHING THREE OF THE FOUR PILLARS THAT SUPPORT THE ROOF IS A SIMPLE TASK FOR SUPERMAN!
CONTINUE WITH YOUR PEACE NEGOTIATIONS OR I'LL SMASH THE RE-MAINING PILLAR--BRINGING THE ENTIRE ROOF DOWN ON YOU!
IF WE VALUE OUR LIVES, WE'VE GOT TO DO AS HE SAYS!
NO, DON'T!
1939, McClure Newspaper Syndicate
AND SO THE DISCUSSION IS FORCIBLY CON-TINUED UNDER THE WATCHFUL EYES OF SUPERMAN!
GO ON! SAY THAT YOUR DEMANDS ARE SELFISH AND ABSURD!
AND I FIND THE REMAINDER OF YOUR TERMS ACCEPTABLE!
I--ER WITHDRAW MY ABSURD DEMANDS
GENTLEMEN, SINCE YOU'VE REACHED AN AMICABLE AGREEMENT, WE CAN ALL SIGN THE PEACE TREATY!
SHORTLY AFTER, THE NEGOTIATIONS COMMIT-TEE MAKES AN IMPORTANT ANNOUNCEMENT TO CHEERING THRONGS...
THE WAR IS OVER! THE COMMITTEE HAS AGREED ON PEACE!

DISAPPEARING DURING THE EXCITEMENT, SUPERMAN DONS CIVILIAN GARMENTS AND WALKS THRU THE REJOICING CITY TO THE AIRPORT.
AND TO THINK THAT JUST A FEW MINUTES AGO THESE HAPPY PEOPLE WERE UNDER THE DREAD SHADOW OF WAR!
BARTOW AND HIS FRIENDS -- ABOUT TO RETURN TO THE UNITED STATES! HOW FORTUNATE... FOR ME!
AMERICAN TELEGRAPH
GEORGE TAYLOR, EDITOR, DAILY STAR, METROPOLIS, N.Y.
BORAVIAN CIVIL WAR ENDS IN TRUCE. RETURNING ON AIRLINER 7-X WITH MURDERERS OF RUNYAN. MEET US AT AIRPORT WITH POLICE.
CLARK KENT
1939, McClure Newspaper Syndicate
WITH THE PLANE ABOUT TO LEAVE IN A FEW MOMENTS, CLARK HURRIEDLY DISPATCHES A TELEGRAM...
MY EDITOR OUGHT TO BE TICKLED TO GET THAT!

TOWARD THE U.S. WINGS THE GREAT BORAVIAN AIRLINER
1939, McClure Newspaper Syndicate
WITHIN IT, THRU THE LONG HOURS OF THE VOYAGE, CLARK KEEPS BARTOW'S MEN UNDER SURVEILLANCE
WHAT'S THE MATTER WITH YOU? WE'VE A FORTUNE IN CASH ON US AND YOU PERSIST IN ACTING JITTERY!
I CAN'T HELP IT-- WHEN I THINK OF SUPERMAN STILL BEING ALIVE.
OH, SNAP OUT OF IT!
AS METROPOLIS IS REACHED...
YOU'RE UNDER ARREST FOR THE MURDER OF ADULPHUS RUNYAN!
BUT--BUT THERE MUST BE SOME MISTAKE! WHO MAKES THIS RIDICULOUS CHARGE?
AIRLINES
I DO! -- AND YOU WON'T THINK IT SO RIDICULOUS WHEN A COURT OF LAW MAKES YOU PAY FOR YOUR CRIME!

NICE GOING, CLARK! NOW GET DOWN TO THE OFFICE AND TURN OUT THE STORY BEFORE ANOTHER PAPER SCOOPS US!
RIGHTO!
DAYS LATER -- KENT TAKES THE WITNESS STAND . . .
AND I DISTINCTL, OVERHEARD BARTOW THREATENING RUNYAN'S LIFE!
THE RACKETEERS FRENZIEDLY SEEK TO PIN THE RAP ON EACH OTHER . . .
HE DID IT! -- I SAW HIM SHOOT RUNYAN!
THAT'S A LIE! YOU DID IT YOURSELF!
1939, McClure Newspaper Syndicate
. . . AND AS A RESULT, RECEIVE A SEVERE PENALTY
I HEREBY SENTENCE ALL THREE OF YOU TO DIE IN THE ELECTRIC CHAIR!

CONGRATULATIONS, CLARK! YOU WERE THE SENSATION OF THE TRIAL!
AND DID YOU SCORE AN EXCLUSIVE ON THAT WAR STORY!
WELL, LOIS? HAS YOUR OPINION OF ME IMPROVED ANY?
IN MY OPINION YOUR SCOOP WAS LUCK--JUST PURE ACCIDENTAL LUCK!
YOUR ADMIRATION OVERWHELMS ME!
CHIEF WANTS TO SEE YOU, CLARK!
WHEN CLARK ENTERS TAYLOR'S OFFICE...
YOU COVERED THE WAR WELL--BUT WHAT ABOUT THE RUNYAN FORMULA?
YOU'VE GOT ME, THERE! I DON'T KNOW A THING ABOUT IT!
1939, McClure Newspaper Syndicate
LATER...
AND THAT'S THE END OF THE FORMULA! IT'S TOO DEADLY TO BE PERMITTED TO EXIST!

EPISODE SEVEN
SUPERMAN AND THE RUNAWAY

DAYBREAK -- A SMALL FIGURE STEALTHILY SLIPS FROM THE STATE ORPHANAGE'S DORMITORY. . .
SH-HH!— WANTA GIVE ME AWAY?
SO-LONG! I GUESS I WON'T BE SEEIN' YA ANY MORE!
STATE ORPHANAGE
GOSH! IT'S HOT! . . . W-WISH I COULDA ET SOMETHIN' BEFORE I LEFT!
McClure Newspaper Syndicate 127
OVERCOME BY HUNGER, FATIGUE, AND HEAT, THE CHILD COLLAPSES. . .
OH-HHH!

AS CLARK KENT, ACE DAILY STAR REPORTER, WALKS TO WORK, HE SIGHTS. . .
GOOD GRIEF!
SWIFTLY REMOVING HIS OUTER GARMENTS, CLARK IS TRANSFORMED INTO THE DYNAMIC MAN OF TOMORROW: SUPERMAN!
NOT AN INSTANT TO LOSE!
I'VE GOT TO REACH THAT BOY IN TIME!
McClure Newspaper Syndicate 128

RACING AT A TERRIFIC RATE OF SPEED, SUPERMAN OVERTAKES THE TRAIN . . .
. . . RACES NECK-AND-NECK! . . .
McClure Newspaper Syndicate
. . . PASSES IT. . !!
. . . . AND LEAPS TO THE BOY'S SIDE! ON HURTLES THE TRAIN -- NOW, ONLY A FEW FEET AWAY!
129

DOWN UPON A HELPLESS, UNCONSCIOUS CHILD AND HIS RESCUER, RACES THE PONDEROUS TRAIN . . . .
TOO LATE FOR ME TO STOP! —THEY HAVEN'T A CHANCE!
McClure Newspaper Syndicate
SNATCHING UP THE BOY, SUPERMAN TAKES A GIANT LEAP THAT CARRIES THEM TO SAFETY!
130
AS THE TRAIN GRINDS TO A HALT, EXCITED PASSENGERS AND TRAINMEN POUR OUT!
THAT WAS THE MOST AMAZING RESCUE I EVER WITNESSED! BUT I STILL CAN'T BELIEVE MY SENSES!
W-WHERE ARE THEY?
GONE! THEY LEAPED COMPLETELY OUT OF SIGHT!

A TREMENDOUS JUMP CARRIES SUPERMAN FAR FROM THE SCENE OF HIS DARING RESCUE!
JUST AS HE AGAIN ASSUMES HIS IDENTITY AS CLARK KENT, THE CHILD REVIVES.
W-WHAT H-HAPPENED?
NEVER MIND,— BUT WHAT MADE YOU PASS OUT LIKE YOU DID?
HUNGER. I HAVEN'T EATEN IN TWO DAYS!
WE'LL SOON FIX THAT! COME WITH ME!
JUST LOOK AT YOU GULP DOWN THAT FOOD! YOU MUST BE *STARVING!*
MM-MM— YOU SAID IT!
McClure Newspaper Syndicate
WELL, G'BYE! AN' THANKS FER THAT SWELL FEED, MISTER!
WAIT! MIND ANSWERING A FEW QUESTIONS?
LUNCH
131

I'M CLARK KENT, REPORTER ON THE *DAILY STAR*. WHAT'S YOUR NAME, SON?
FRANKIE, SIR. FRANKIE DENNIS!
132
WHERE DO YOU LIVE, FRANKIE?— I'LL TAKE YOU HOME!
LEMME GO! I AIN'T GOTTA HOME, I TELL YA!
YOU'RE NOT RUNNING AWAY FROM HOME, ARE YOU, FRANKIE?
HOME? YA WOULDN'T CALL A PLACE WHERE TH' SUPERINTENDENT BEATS, AN' STARVES, AN' SLAVEDRIVES YA "HOME," WOULD YA?
McClure Newspaper Syndicate
I WON'T GO BACK TO THAT STATE ORPHANAGE! DO YA HEAR-- I WON'T!
("—STATE ORPHANAGE, EH? —HM-MM! SOUNDS LIKE THERE MIGHT BE A STORY HERE!—")

TELL ME: WHAT DO THEY DO TO YOU AT THE ORPHANAGE?
SUPERINTENDENT LYMAN GIVES US KIDS FOOD NOT FIT T'EAT, HIRES US OUT FER HARD LABOR, BEATS US -- AN' MAKES US SCRUB FLOORS FER HOURS AN HOURS!
THAT'S A PRETTY NASTY STATE OF AFFAIRS! -- CERTAIN YOU'RE NOT LYING?
IT'S TRUE -- EVERY WORD OF IT! PLEASE DON'T MAKE ME GO BACK TO THAT ORPHANAGE, MISTER!
133
LOOK -- IF WHAT YOU SAY IS TRUE, I MAY BE ABLE TO HELP, BUT I WOULDN'T DO ANYTHING WITHOUT YOUR ASSISTANCE!
ME HELP? WHY IF I WAS TO GO BACK NOW TH' SUPERINTENDENT WOULD HAVE IT IN FER ME TWICE AS MUCH!
BUT THINK OF ALL THE OTHER CHILDREN BACK THERE AT THE ORPHANAGE! SURELY, YOU'RE NOT GOING TO LET THEM DOWN JUST BECAUSE YOU'RE AFRAID?
McClure Newspaper Syndicate

B-BUT HOW WOULD MY GOIN' BACK TO TH' ORPHANAGE HELP TH' KIDS?
YOU WOULD BE MY UNDERCOVER MAN -- A SORT OF DETECTIVE -- AND REPORT BACK TO ME ALL OF THE SUPERINTENDENT'S UNJUST ACTS.
134
FRANKIE'S INNER STRUGGLE IS REFLECTED UPON HIS FEATURES! -- TO RETURN TO THAT LOATHSOME SLAVERY ??... OR CLING TO HIS PRECIOUS FREEDOM ??...
?
I'LL DO IT! I-I'LL GO BACK!
STOUT FELLOW! -- I KNEW YOU WOULDN'T ABANDON YOUR FRIENDS!
BUT WHEN THEY REACH THE STATE ORPHANAGE...
YOU'RE TREMBLING, FRANKIE! DON'T! THERE'S NO LONGER ANYTHING TO BE FRIGHTENED OF!
I KNOW THAT ALL RIGHT, BUT MY KNEES DON'T!
McClure Newspaper Syndicate

WHAT DO YOU W-- FRANKIE! —FRANKIE DENNIS!
DON'T HIT ME, MISTER LYMAN! -- DON'T!
YOU BLASTED LITTLE RUNAWAY —I'LL--!
135
TAKE YOUR HANDS OFF THAT BOY!!
McClure Newspaper Syndicate
WHO ARE YOU? HOW DARE YOU TELL ME HOW TO RUN MY AFFAIRS?
I'M REPORTER KENT, OF THE DAILY STAR —I PERSUADED THIS BOY TO RETURN HERE!
A REPORTER, EH? --ER--THAT'S DIFFERENT... PLEASE EXCUSE MY LITTLE BURST OF TEMPER! BUT WHEN A BOY REPAYS MY GENTLE KINDNESS BY RUNNING AWAY, IT IRKS ME!

I LOVE MY MISCHIEVOUS LITTLE CHARGES, BUT THIS LITTLE TYKE HAS HAD ME WORRIED TO DEATH BY HIS DISAPPEARANCE! YOU UNDERSTAND, DON'T YOU?
QUITE! WELL, I MUST LEAVE YOU NOW!
McClure Newspaper Syndicate
DO RETURN ANY TIME YOU DESIRE! WE'RE ALWAYS PLEASED TO HAVE VISITORS, AREN'T WE, FRANKIE?
Y-YES!
THANKS FOR THE INVITATION! I MAY TAKE YOU UP!
THE KID MIGHT HAVE BEEN LYING -- AND YET THAT SUPERINTENDENT IMPRESSES ME AS BEING A WILY RASCAL!
WHAT DID YOU SPILL TO THAT SNOOPING REPORTER? TELL ME-- OR I'LL SMASH THAT PASTY FACE OF YOURS! TELL ME! -- TELL ME!
NOTHIN'! HONEST! -- I DIDN'T TELL HIM NOTHIN'! PLEASE! LET ME GO!
136

WHEN CLARK REACHES THE *DAILY STAR* . . .
HOW ABOUT HAVING LUNCH WITH ME TODAY, LOIS ?
SORRY—NOT INTERESTED!
AW, COME ON! --I'M NOT POISON IVY!
FOR ONCE AND ALL, WILL YOU PLEASE LET IT REGISTER IN THAT THICK DOME OF YOURS THAT I DISLIKE YOU HEARTILY! *UNDERSTAND?*
TAYLOR WANTS TO SEE YOU, CLARK!
YOU KNOW THAT SPECTACULAR RESCUE BY AN UNKNOWN MAN OF THE RUNAWAY FROM THE STATE ORPHANAGE-- --SEE WHAT YOU CAN DIG UP ON IT!
FINE, CHIEF! --I'D LIKE TO COVER IT!-- I'VE GOT A HUNCH ABOUT CONDITIONS IN THAT INSTITUTION!— WHY NOT HAVE LOIS HELP ME COVER THAT ANGLE?
137. McClure Newspaper Syndicate
SOUNDS SWELL!
('—WHAT A BREAK!— HO! HO! SHE'LL HAVE TO BEAR MY COMPANY NOW, WHETHER SHE WANTS TO OR NOT!—')

LOIS, CLARK HAS REASON TO BELIEVE THERE'S DIRTY WORK GOING ON AT THE STATE ORPHANAGE. THIS MAY TURN OUT TO BE A BIG STORY. GIVE HIM YOUR COMPLETE COOPERATION.
I'M SURE SHE'LL BE ONLY *TOO* DELIGHTED!
DELIGHTED!— WHY . . . !
I'M GOING WITH YOU ONLY BECAUSE I'M FORCED TO-- AND DON'T YOU FORGET IT!
WHAT DIFFERENCE DOES THAT MAKE AS LONG AS WE'RE-- *ALONE?*
McClure Newspaper Syndicate
WAIT UP!
HOLD IT, CLARK!
JUST A MINUTE!
?
138
REPORTERS-- FROM THE RIVAL PAPERS!
DID YOU SAY *ALONE?*

HELLO...IF IT ISN'T MY BELOVED CONTEMPORARIES! NICE DAY, ISN'T IT? -- WELL, SEE YOU LATER!
NOT SO FAST! —WHAT'S THE HURRY?
CAN'T CLARK AND I HAVE A LUNCHEON DATE WITHOUT YOU RIVAL NEWS-HOUNDS BUTTING IN?
LUNCHEON DATE, EH? YOU COULDN'T POSSIBLY BE ON THE TRACK OF AN IMPORTANT NEWS STORY, COULD YOU?
WITH YOUR IMAGINATION, YOU SHOULD WRITE FICTION!
AW, COME ON CLARKSIE, DON'T BE SELFISH! WHAT'S UP?
NOTHING, I TELL YOU!
WELL...MAYBE YOU'RE RIGHT!
WHEW! — I THOUGHT WE'D NEVER GET RID OF THEM!
IM NOT SO POSITIVE WE HAVE!
McClure Newspaper Syndicate
139

WHAT DO YOU MEAN YOU'RE NOT SO POSITIVE WE DODGED THOSE REPORTERS?
TAKE A LOOK BACK...AND SEE FOR YOURSELF!
CLOSELY IN PURSUIT OF THEIR CAB IS ANOTHER TAXI!...
McClure Newspaper Syndicate 140
THEY'RE TRAILING US!
WE'RE BEING FOLLOWED! SHAKE OFF THE TAXI BEHIND US AND THERE'S A FIVE SPOT IN IT FOR YOU.
LEAVE IT TO ME!
UNEXPECTEDLY, CLARK'S TAXI SWERVES SHARPLY INTO AN ALLEY.
THAT OUGHT TO DO THE TRICK!

GOSH, I THOUGHT WE'D NEVER SHAKE OFF THOSE REPORTERS!
BUT WE DID!
McClure Newspaper Syndicate
LATER. . . WHEN THEY REACH THE STATE ORPHANAGE . . .
REMEMBER, LOIS! GIVE LYMAN NO REASON TO SUSPECT YOU BELIEVE ANYTHING AMISS!
I CAN JUST PICTURE THE FACES OF THOSE REPORTERS WHEN THEY READ OUR SCOOP IN THE DAILY STAR!
HI, CLARK!
REMEMBER US?
LUNCHEON DATE, EH?
THE REPORTERS!
113
141

OF ALL THE DIRTY TRICKS -- YOU DELIBERATELY FOLLOWED US!
YOU KNOW THE OLD SAYING: "ALL'S FAIR IN LOVE, WAR, AND GATHERING THE NEWS*!
QUIT TRYING TO HOLD OUT ON US! WHAT'S GOING ON HERE AT THE ORPHANAGE?
NOTHING MUCH! THIS IS GOING TO BE JUST A ROUTINE FEATURE STORY!
THAT'S WHY WE DIDN'T BOTHER TO TELL YOU OF IT!
WHEN A RIVAL REPORTER GETS MAGNANIMOUS, IT AROUSES THE SUSPICIOUS STREAK IN ME.
McClure Newspaper Syndicate
WHY DOESN'T SOMEONE ANSWER THE DOOR? YOU'VE BEEN RINGING IT LONG ENOUGH.
THE DOORBELL ISN'T OUT OF ORDER... CAN HEAR IT RINGING.
NEWSPAPERMEN! —I'VE GOT TO THINK FAST!
142

NOT A MINUTE TO LOSE! I'LL HAVE TO LET THOSE REPORTERS IN, AND IF THEY WITNESS CONDITIONS AS THEY REALLY ARE...!
McClure Newspaper Syndicate
STOP WORKING, ALL OF YOU...PUT YOUR MATERIALS AWAY AND BEGIN TO PLAY GAMES!
Y-YESSIR, MR. LYMAN!
IF THESE SNOOPING REPORTERS QUESTION YOU, REMEMBER: YOU LOVE THE HOME, YOU'RE PLEASED WITH CONDITIONS — AND ANY-ONE WHO SAYS DIFFERENT WILL BE SEVERELY PUNISHED. GET ME?
143
COME RIGHT IN AND PLEASE PARDON THE DELAY! I WAS BUSY FILLING OUT SOME REPORTS.
THEY MUST HAVE BEEN INTERESTING REPORTS — WE'VE BEEN RINGING FOR NEARLY FIVE MINUTES!

AND WHAT CAN I DO FOR YOU?
DO YOU MIND LETTING US LOOK OVER THE ORPHANAGE -- OUR EDITORS THINK READERS WOULD BE INTERESTED IN LEARNING OF YOUR WORK!
I'LL BE ONLY TOO PLEASED TO SHOW YOU THE PLACE. FOLLOW ME!
WE'LL JUST HAVE TO MAKE THE BEST OF IT!
HOW CAN WE CARRY ON OUR INVESTIGATION WITH THE OTHER REPORTERS AROUND?
SEE HOW CONTENTED THEY ARE -- HOW HAPPILY THEY PLAY. THEY'VE ALL THE COMFORTS OF A REAL HOME!
IT'S A FINE JOB YOU'RE DOING, LYMAN!
JUST LOOK AT THE FUN THEY'RE HAVING!
144 McClure Newspaper Syndicate
I LOVE THEM ALL AS THOUGH THEY WERE MY OWN CHILDREN. ("— HA! HA! — HOW SIMPLE IT IS TO PULL THE WOOL OVER THEIR EYES-")
MAY I QUOTE THAT STATE-MENT, SIR? ("—I STILL DON'T TRUST HIM!—")

HELLO, LITTLE GIRL! WHAT'S YOUR NAME? -- HOW DO YOU LIKE IT HERE?
I—I LIKE IT FINE. MR. LYMAN'S VERY GOOD TO US. HE NEVER HITS US, OR ANYTHING!
JUST LOOK AT THAT BRUISE ON YOUR ARM. HOW DID YOU GET IT?
I—I . . .
DON'T BE FRIGHTENED. TELL ME: *WHERE DID YOU GET THAT MARK?*
I -- I FELL DOWN!
145
THE CHILD'S TREMBLING AS THOUGH SHE WERE IN TERRIBLE FEAR OF SOMETHING OR SOMEONE. I WONDER. DID SHE FALL OR WAS SHE *STRUCK*?
McClure Newspaper Syndicate

LOOKING THROUGH THE ORPHANS' QUARTER, LOIS FINDS A CHILD CONFINED TO ITS BED . . .
YOU LOOK WAN AND WEAK! — WHAT'S WRONG WITH YOU?
I GUESS I'M TIRED OUT FROM PLAYIN' TOO MUCH.
YOU'RE SURE THERE'S NO OTHER REASON?
POSITIVE, MISS! ("—I DON'T DARE TELL HER I'M LAID UP FROM WORKIN' TOO HARD—")
PS-ST! — MR. KENT!
146
WHAT IS IT FRANKIE?
THERE'S SOMETHIN' I GOTTA TELL YA AN' I HAVEN'T MUCH TIME!
McClure Newspaper Syndicate
146

WHAT DO YOU WISH TO TELL ME, FRANKIE ?
ITS ABOUT MR. LYMAN HE WARNED THE KIDS THA **OMIGOSH!**
WHAT'S WRONG? WHY DON'T YOU GO ON ?
I GOT NOTHIN' TO TELL YA . . . HONEST, I AIN'T!
McClure Newspaper Syndicate 147
IF YOU WISHED TO TELL MR. KENT SOMETHING, FRANKIE, — GO RIGHT AHEAD!
N-NO! THERE AIN'T NOTHIN' I GOTTA SAY!
WELL, ARE YOU SATISFIED WITH YOUR INSPECT-ION ?
QUITE. I GUESS WE MIGHT AS WELL LEAVE NOW. ("— I WONDER WHAT FRANKIE WAS GOING TO REVEAL?-")

SO THAT WAS YOUR GREAT YARN
NOT SO HOT, IF YOU ASK ME!
YOU SEE, IT'S JUST AS I TOLD YOU. NOTHING BUT A MEDIOCRE FEATURE STORY!
WELL, WHATEVER BE-CAME OF YOUR HUNCH THAT THERE WAS SOME-THING AMISS AT THE STATE ORPHANAGE?
I STILL THINK THAT SUPER-INTENDENT ISN'T ON THE LEVEL!
AS SOON AS THE REPORTERS LEAVE --
STOP THAT LOAFING. ALL OF YOU -- BACK TO WORK! — AND AS FOR YOU . . .
DON'T! YOU'RE HURT-ING ME!
McClure Newspaper Syndicate
I'LL JUST LOCK YOU HERE IN THE ATTIC UNTIL YOU LEARN TO KEEP THAT TRAP OF YOURS SHUT!
148

THAT EVENING . . . CLARK REMOVES HIS OUTER GARMENTS REVEALING HIS TRUE IDENTITY AS SUPERMAN, CHAMPION OF THE OPPRESSED . . .
THERE'S MORE TO THAT ORPHANAGE THAN MEETS THE EYE . . .
AND I INTEND TO GET DOWN TO THE BOTTOM OF IT !
A SCIENTIFIC EXPLANATION OF SUPERMAN'S SUPER-STRENGTH
SUPERMAN WAS BORN ON A PLANET WHOSE GRAVITATIONAL PULL WAS MUCH GREATER THAN THAT OF OUR EARTH'S -- THUS HIS INCREDIBLE FEATS OF STRENGTH!
EARTH
KRYPTON
McClure Newspaper Syndicate

HIGH OVER THE CITY STREAKS A FANTASTIC PHANTOM OF THE NIGHT: SUPERMAN!
DOWN HE HURTLES TO THE SIDE OF THE STATE ORPHANAGE
McClure Newspaper Syndicate
IT'S LYMAN . . . CHECKING OVER HIS BOOKS !
151
WHAT THOSE REPORTERS WOULDN'T GIVE TO SEE THIS SECRET ACCOUNT-BOOK!

LYMAN GLOATS OVER THE FIGURES OF HIS GRAFTING, UNAWARE HE IS BEING OBSERVED BY SUPERMAN . . .
NOT BAD! NOT BAD AT ALL! SOON I'LL HAVE ENOUGH TO CLEAR OUT OF HERE!
AT HOME, LOIS TOSSES. . . TURNS . . .
IT'S NO USE TRYING. . . I CAN'T SLEEP! — IS THAT ORPHANAGE RUN ON THE LEVEL?
AND LOCKED IN THE ORPHANAGE ATTIC . . .
W-WHERE AM I ?
152
McClure Newspaper Syndicate
OPEN THIS DOOR! LEMME OUT! — I WON'T STOP YELLIN' TILL YA LET ME OUT!

WHAT'S THAT NOISE?
McClure Newspaper Syndicate
I'LL SHOW 'IM! — LET ME OUT OR I'LL WRECK TH' PLACE!
IT'S THAT BRAT UP IN THE ATTIC! I'LL FIX HIM!
HE'S GONE! — — NOW'S MY CHANCE TO LOOK OVER THOSE ACCOUNT BOOKS!
153

THESE ENTRIES INDICATE THE PRICES LYMAN PAID FOR FOOD PURCHASED FROM THE *STAR GROCERIES COMPANY*. THEY LOOK UNUSUALLY HIGH TO ME!
I'LL JUST CHECK UP!
154
McClure Newspaper Syndicate
I'M PROBABLY BEING AN UTTER FOOL, BUT I'M GOING BACK TO THE STATE ORPHANAGE TO LOOK IT OVER WHILE THE SUPERINTENDENT IS OFF-GUARD!
YOU LITTLE TROUBLE-MAKER! I'LL LASH THE HIDE OFF YOU!
NO!-- DON'T!

ON THE ROOF OF THE *STAR GROCERIES COMPANY*, *SUPERMAN* PRIES OPEN THE SKYLIGHT, ENTERS . . .
McClure Newspaper Syndicate
155
. . . THEN FORCES THE COMPANY'S STEEL FILES!
I DISLIKE WRECKING THEIR EQUIPMENT BUT IT'S NECESSARY!
THE FIGURES IN THESE TWO BOOKS DIFFER! LYMAN IS GRAFTING OUTRAGEOUSLY ON THE FOOD BILL!
I'VE ALL THE PROOF I NEED! NOW TO GIVE LYMAN WHAT HE DESERVES!

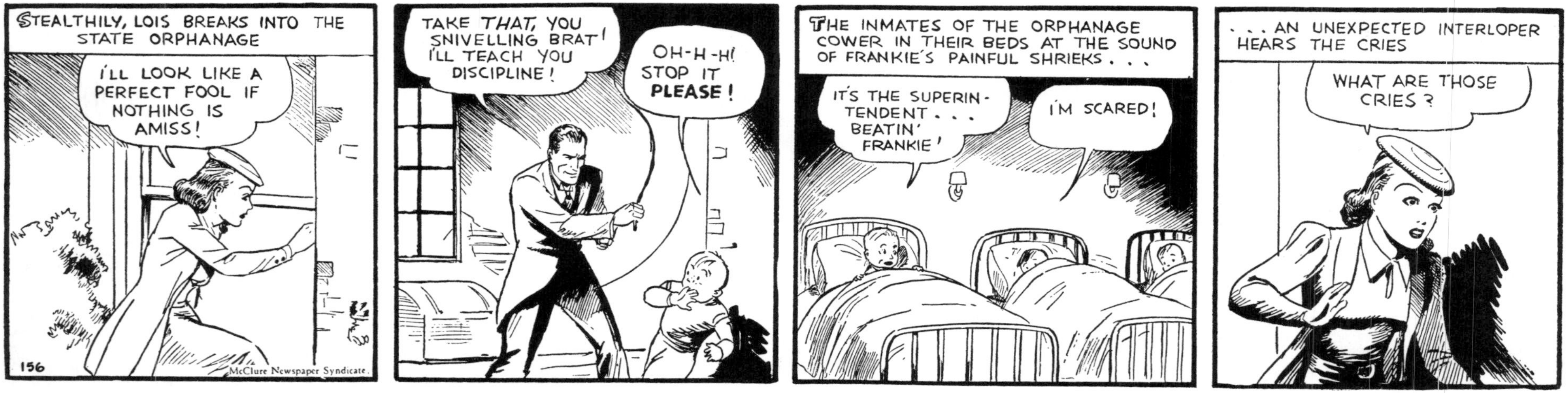
STEALTHILY, LOIS BREAKS INTO THE STATE ORPHANAGE
I'LL LOOK LIKE A PERFECT FOOL IF NOTHING IS AMISS!
156
McClure Newspaper Syndicate.
TAKE THAT, YOU SNIVELLING BRAT! I'LL TEACH YOU DISCIPLINE!
OH-H-H! STOP IT PLEASE!
THE INMATES OF THE ORPHANAGE COWER IN THEIR BEDS AT THE SOUND OF FRANKIE'S PAINFUL SHRIEKS . . .
IT'S THE SUPERIN-TENDENT . . . BEATIN' FRANKIE!
I'M SCARED!
. . . AN UNEXPECTED INTERLOPER HEARS THE CRIES
WHAT ARE THOSE CRIES ?

STOP IT!
YOU! YOU'RE ONE OF THOSE SNOOP-ING REPORTERS! WHAT ARE YOU DOING HERE ?
McClure Newspaper Syndicate
I SUSPECTED YOU OF JUST THIS SORT OF THING! I'M GOING TO PRINT WHAT I'VE SEEN . . !
OUT OF MY WAY!
YOU'LL NEVER PRINT THAT STORY! —I'LL KILL YOU FIRST!
YOU'RE INSANE! OPEN THE DOOR!
157

THAT GIRL'S STORY WILL START AN INVEST IGATION AND RUIN EVERYTHING!
McClure Newspaper Syndicate
158
LUCKILY, THERE'S ENOUGH CASH FOR A QUICK GET-AWAY! —THERE'S NOT A MOMENT TO LOSE!
BUT FIRST I'VE GOT TO MAKE CERTAIN THAT GIRL WILL NEVER TALK!
LAUGHING WITH MAD GLEE, THE CRAZED SUPER-INTENDENT SETS FIRE TO THE ORPHANAGE
HO! HO!--I'LL BURN IT DOWN TO THE GROUND! THEY'LL NEVER CATCH ME! I'LL SKIP THE COUNTRY!

CRAZED WITH FEAR, THE TERRIFIED OCCUPANTS OF THE BLAZING ORPHANAGE RUSH OUT INTO THE COLD NIGHT . . . .
McClure Newspaper Syndicate
WE CAN'T! —THE DOOR WON'T BUDGE! —I CAN —HARDLY BREATHE!
TH' PLACE IS ON FIRE! — WE GOTTA GET OUT!
NO ONE NOTICED ME! THE MOMENT I REACH THAT CAR I'LL BE ON MY WAY TO SOUTH AMERICA AND A LIFE OF LUXURY!
THE SUPERINTENDENT . . .RUSHING FROM THE BURNING ORPHANAGE! THE COWARD'S GONE INSANE!
159

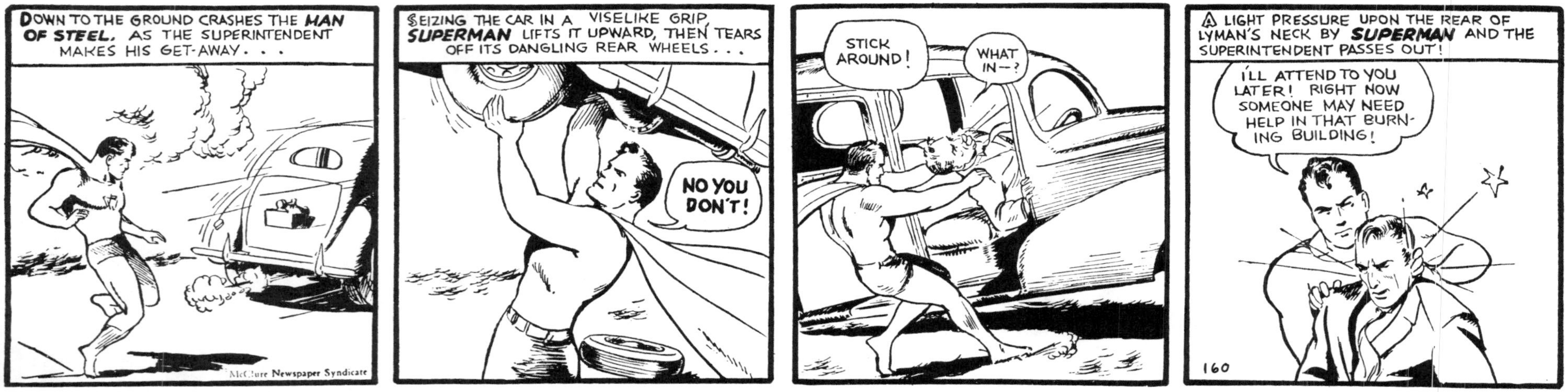
DOWN TO THE GROUND CRASHES THE MAN OF STEEL, AS THE SUPERINTENDENT MAKES HIS GET-AWAY . . .
McClure Newspaper Syndicate
SEIZING THE CAR IN A VISELIKE GRIP, SUPERMAN LIFTS IT UPWARD, THEN TEARS OFF ITS DANGLING REAR WHEELS . . .
NO YOU DON'T!
STICK AROUND!
WHAT IN--?
A LIGHT PRESSURE UPON THE REAR OF LYMAN'S NECK BY SUPERMAN AND THE SUPERINTENDENT PASSES OUT!
I'LL ATTEND TO YOU LATER! RIGHT NOW SOMEONE MAY NEED HELP IN THAT BURNING BUILDING!
160

SHE'S UNCONSCIOUS FROM THE SMOKE! HELP! HELP!
FRANKIE -- TRAPPED IN THE ATTIC!
161
GRAB HOLD. WE'VE GOT TO JUMP BEFORE THE BUILDING COLLAPSES!
WAIT! THERE'S A GIRL IN THE ROOM!
DOWN FROM THE CRASHING BUILDING LEAPS SUPERMAN, LOIS AND FRANKIE SAFELY IN HIS ARMS . . .
W-WHAT HAPPENED? HOW DID I GET HERE?
THAT GUY WE'VE READ SO MUCH ABOUT SUPERMAN ... HE BROUGHT US DOWN SAFELY--THEN BEAT IT!
McClure Newspaper Syndicate

YOU SAY THAT SUPERMAN SAVED US FROM DEATH IN THE BURNING BUILDING!
YES! GOSH! IS HE STRONG! WOTTA MAN!
LOIS! — THANK GOODNESS YOU'RE SAFE!
162
McClure Newspaper Syndicate
ARREST THAT MAN-- HE SET FIRE TO THE ORPHANAGE!
LET ME GO! ... I DIDN'T KNOW WHAT I WAS DOING!
EDITION
The Daily Star
Wire Photo Service
Vol. XXVI. No.
GRAFT, CRUELTY REIG
IN STATE ORPHANAG
by CLARK KENT
SUPERINTENDENT
BOY HERO
CLARK VISITS THE REBUILT STATE ORPHANAGE
WELL, FRANKIE HOW DO YOU AND THE OTHER KIDS LIKE YOUR NEW SUPERINTENDENT?
HE'S SWELL! — AND SO ARE YOU, MR. KENT!

EPISODE EIGHT
ROYAL DEATHPLOT

I FEEL IN A CONCILIATORY MOOD, CLARK. WOULD YOU CARE TO COME OVER FOR DINNER TONIGHT?
I'D BE DELIGHTED!
163. 1939 McClure Newspaper Syndicate
THAT EVENING..
MAKE YOURSELF RIGHT AT HOME WHILE I PUT THE FINISHING TOUCHES TO MY DINNER!
O.K. I'LL TURN ON THE RADIO
ALL READY! -- I'LL BE IN IN A MINUTE.
WE INTERRUPT THE DANCE MUSIC TO ANNOUNCE A STARTLING NEWS BROADCAST!
WONDER WHAT'S UP?

FLASH! A DISTRESS SIGNAL HAS JUST BEEN BROADCAST FROM THE ROYAL YACHT, MILAN, ENROUTE TO AMERICA FROM RANGORIA WITH KING BORU AND HIS DAUGHTER PRINCESS TANIA ABOARD!
AN UNKNOWN SUB-MARINE IS TRAILING THE MILAN AND ITS TWO CONVOY SHIPS. IMPENDING VIOLENCE IS FEARED!
WHEW!
ONE LITHE STEP BRINGS THE DAILY STAR REPORTER TO LOIS' WINDOW SILL... NEXT INSTANT, HE STEPS OUT INTO EMPTY SPACE, AND VANISHES FROM VIEW...
164 1939 McClure Newspaper Syndicate
WELL, HERE WE AR--- WHAT TH'-? HE'S GONE!

NOW FOR THE ROOF!
165
LOIS WILL BURN WHEN SHE FINDS I'M GONE, BUT THERE ARE MORE IM-PORTANT THINGS AT STAKE!
I'LL PICK THESE UP ON MY NEXT VISIT!
A TREMENDOUS BURST FROM SUPERMAN'S MIGHTY MUSCLES, AND HE SOARS OUT OVER THE CITY....
1939 McClure Newspaper Syndicate

WHAM! - STEELY MUSCLES CUSHION THE SHOCK OF A HUNDRED FOOT DROP....
I'VE A PRETTY GOOD IDEA OF THE MILAN'S PROBABLE LOCATION AT THIS MOMENT!
166
...THEN THE MAN OF TOMORROW RACES ALONG AT AN INCREDIBLE SPEED!
I HOPE I DON'T ARRIVE TOO LATE!
1939 McClure Newspaper Syndicate
FIVE MINUTES LATER...THE WIERD FIGURE WHIZZES DOWN OVER DOCKED STEAMERS IN A CLEAN CUT DIVE...
AT THIS RATE I SHOULD REACH THE MILAN IN A FEW MINUTES!

ABOARD THE MILAN . . .
WHY DON'T THE CONVOYS DO SOMETHING?
THEY'VE WARNED THE SUBMARINE THAT IF IT DOESN'T MOVE OFF, THEY'LL FIRE, YOUR MAJESTY
I'M SO EXCITED!
SUPERMAN SWIMS SO SWIFTLY THAT HE OVERTAKES AND PASSES SPEEDING LAUNCHES-
167
. . . SHORTLY AFTER HE ARRIVES UPON THE SCENE OF THE TENSE OCEAN DRAMA . . .
. . JUST IN TIME TO WITNESS THE TORPEDOING OF A CONVOY SHIP!

OUR REMAINING CONVOY SHIP-- TORPEDOED!
WE'RE DOOMED! NOW THE SUBMARINE IS FREE TO ATTACK US!
WITHIN THE UNKNOWN SUB . . . .
FIRE!
168
BEFORE SUPERMAN'S SHOCKED GAZE, A TORPEDO SPEEDS TOWARD THE MILAN, ON ITS GRIM ERRAND OF DEATH!

DIRECTLY TOWARD THE MILAN GLIDES A MURDEROUS TORPEDO...
SWIMMING AT TERRIFIC SPEED, SUPERMAN BRIDGES THE SPACE BETWEEN IT AND HIMSELF...
..A SHARP THRUST OF HIS ARM SENDS IT WHIRLING...
Copyright 1939, McClure Newspaper Syndicate
...AND THE TORPEDO NARROWLY MISSES ITS TARGET!
169

WHEW! THAT WAS CLOSE! A FEW INCHES OVER AND...!
BUT THE DANGER IS NOT OVER! ANOTHER TORPEDO IS LAUNCHED TOWARD THE MILAN...
HERE I GO AGAIN!
MAN AND TORPEDO MEET....
Copyright 1939, McClure Newspaper Syndicate
170
AMIDST A TERRIFIC EXPLOSION!

ABOARD THE MILAN . . .
LOOK! THERE'S NO LONGER ANY SIGN OF HIM!
IT WAS INCREDIBLE! A MAN..RACING A TORPEDO.. HEADING IT OFF!
INCREDIBLE? - - - IT WAS MAGNIFICENT!
Copyright 1939, McClure Newspaper Syndicate
MILAN
THE SUB RISES . . . .
DESTROY THAT VESSEL! SHOW IT NO MERCY!
. . AND OPENS FIRE!
WE HAVEN'T A CHANCE! THEY'LL SINK US!
NOTHING CAN SAVE US, NOW--EXCEPT A MIRACLE!
171

AS THE SUBMARINE CONTINUES TO FIRE STEADILY AT THE STRICKEN ROYAL YACHT, THE DESTRUCTION OF THE MILAN APPEARS CERTAIN . . .
ONTO THE SUB CLIMBS--SUPERMAN! HIS IMPENETRABLE SKIN AND AMAZING PHYSICAL STRUCTURE HAVE ENABLED HIM TO ESCAPE THE EXPLOSION UNSCATHED!
172
CONTINUE FIRING!
YOU WON'T.. IF YOU VALUE YOUR HIDES!
Copyright 1939, McClure Newspaper Syndicate

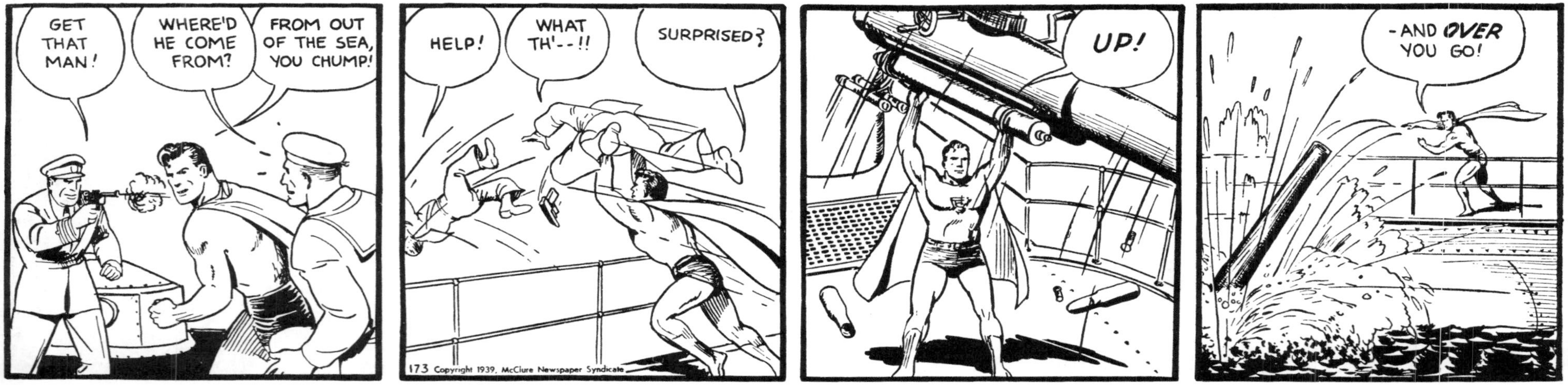
GET THAT MAN!
WHERE'D HE COME FROM?
FROM OUT OF THE SEA, YOU CHUMP!
HELP!
WHAT TH'--!!
SURPRISED?
173 Copyright 1939, McClure Newspaper Syndicate
UP!
-AND OVER YOU GO!

QUICK! NOTIFY OUR SUPERIORS!
Y-YES, SIR!
Copyright 1939, McClure Newspaper Syndicate
"COUNTER-ATTACKED--CAPTURE IMMINENT--WHAT ARE YOUR ORDERS?"
IN A DISTANT OFFICE . . .
TELL THEM TO TAKE NO CHANCES. RATHER THAN RISK WORLDWIDE REPERCUSSIONS IF OUR PLOT WERE EXPOSED--DESTROY THEMSELVES!
174.
ORDERS ARE TO WIPE OUT ALL EVIDENCE!
I---UNDERSTAND..!

AND NOW...THERE ARE SOME MATTERS I'D LIKE TO SETTLE WITH YOU!
KEEP BACK!
Copyright 1939, McClure Newspaper Syndicate
I WARN YOU -- STAY BACK, OR YOU'LL REGRET IT!
SORRY...BUT YOU FAIL TO TERRIFY ME!
WHY DID YOU ATTACK THE MILAN?
YOU'LL NEVER LIVE TO KNOW!
BACK KICKS THE COMMANDER'S FOOT... WHAT IS HIS DESPERATE PLAN?
175.

NO STALLING NOW! TELL ME WHO PROVOKED THIS ATTACK ON THE MILAN.... AND WHY?
YOU'LL NEVER KNOW...BECAUSE THE SECRET WILL DIE WITH US RIGHT HERE AND NOW!
DESPERATELY, THE COMMANDER'S FOOT JABS AT A BUTTON ON THE SUB'S DECK..
Copyright 1939, McClure Newspaper Syndicate 176

IN A DISTANT ROOM, MILES AWAY FROM THE SCENE OF THE SEA DISASTER...
I'VE TRIED CONTACTING THE SUB, SIR... BUT THEY DON'T ANSWER!
IT IS WELL! -THEY HAVE SACRIFICED THEIR LIVES FOR THE CAUSE!
LOOK! THE SUB IS BLOWING UP!
THANK GOD!
BUT THAT BRAVE MAN WHO AIDED US --- THEN HE'S DESTROYED, TOO!
CAUGHT BY THE EXPLOSION'S MIGHTY GRIP, SUPERMAN IS FLUNG, TWISTING AND TURNING INTO THE OCEAN'S DEPTHS...
Copyright 1939, McClure Newspaper Syndicate
177
...STUNNED INTO UNCONSCIOUSNESS, HE DRIFTS SENSELESSLY AT THE MERCY OF AN UNDERWATER CURRENT!

SAFE FROM THE MENACE OF THE UNKNOWN SUBMARINE, THE ROYAL YACHT CONTINUES ON ITS WAY TO THE UNITED STATES...
BUT WHAT PUZZLES ME IS THAT EXHIBITION OF INCREDIBLE STRENGTH. I STILL CAN'T BELIEVE IT!
HOW I'D LIKE TO MEET THAT MAN!
178
AS SUPERMAN REGAINS HIS SENSES, HE STRIKES OUT FOR THE SURFACE...
THERE GOES THE MILAN... WELL, HERE I GO!
Copyright 1939, McClure Newspaper Syndicate

SUPERMAN STREAKS THRU THE WATER AFTER THE DISAPPEARING MILAN . . .
Copyright 1939, McClure Newspaper Syndicate 179
. . . OVERTAKING IT WITHIN A FEW MINUTES!
A MYSTERIOUS CLOAKED FIGURE CLIMBS ONTO THE DECK OF THE MILAN IN THE STILL OF THE NIGHT!
GOSH! — THAT EXPLOSION NEARLY FINISHED ME!

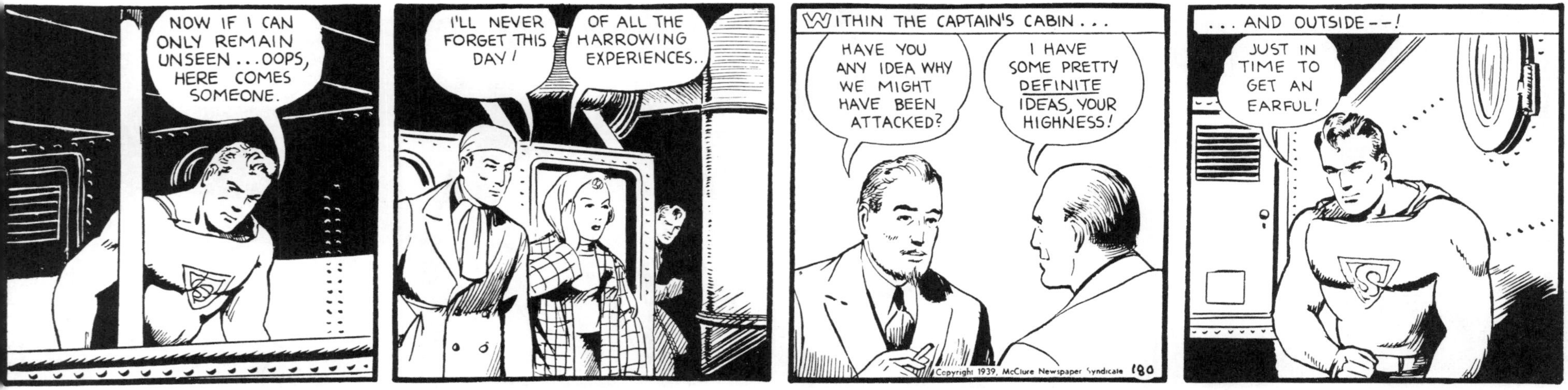
NOW IF I CAN ONLY REMAIN UNSEEN . . . OOPS, HERE COMES SOMEONE.
I'LL NEVER FORGET THIS DAY!
OF ALL THE HARROWING EXPERIENCES . .
WITHIN THE CAPTAIN'S CABIN . . .
HAVE YOU ANY IDEA WHY WE MIGHT HAVE BEEN ATTACKED?
I HAVE SOME PRETTY DEFINITE IDEAS, YOUR HIGHNESS!
Copyright 1939, McClure Newspaper Syndicate 180
. . . AND OUTSIDE - - !
JUST IN TIME TO GET AN EARFUL!

TELL ME, YOUR HIGHNESS... WHAT'S THE PRIMARY PURPOSE OF YOUR VISIT TO THE UNITED STATES?
I HOPE TO ENCOURAGE FRIENDSHIP BETWEEN THE U.S. AND RANGORIA
EXACTLY. NOW WOULDN'T IT FIT IN WITH THE PLANS OF YOUR POLITICAL ENEMIES IF YOU AND YOUR DAUGHTER WERE SLAIN IN AMERICA?
THAT'S IT! THEY HOPE TO CAUSE A SERIOUS RUPTURE BETWEEN THE TWO NATIONS —AND SEIZE THE THRONE!
Copyright 1939, McClure Newspaper Syndicate
THOUGH ENGROSSED IN HIS EAVESDROPPING, SUPERMAN'S SUPER-HEARING WARNS HIM THAT SOMEONE IS STEALING UP FROM BEHIND...
NOT SO FAST!
A GIRL --AND A BEAUTIFUL ONE, AT THAT!
181

SORRY...I DIDN'T MEAN TO MANHANDLE YOU!
YOU... YOU...!
TAKE THAT, CUR!
182
DO YOU REALIZE WHAT YOU HAVE DONE? YOU HAVE LAID HANDS ON PRINCESS TANIA!
I SUPPOSE THAT BEING A PRINCESS GIVES YOU THE PRIVILEGE OF BEING ILL-TEMPERED!
WAIT! I RECOGNIZE YOU NOW! YOU ARE THE BRAVE, INCREDIBLY STRONG MAN WHO SAVED US FROM THAT SUBMARINE!
SUPERMAN, PRINCESS-- AT YOUR SERVICE!
Copyright 1939, McClure Newspaper Syndicate

THE ROYAL HOUSE OF RANGORIA IS DEEPLY INDEBTED TO YOU!
I STRIVE TO CORRECT INJUSTICE WHEREVER I FIND IT!
FORGIVE MY HASTY TEMPER! BELIEVE ME -- I'M SORRY!
YOU'RE FORGIVEN. THAT MAKES US FRIENDS, DOESN'T IT? --WELL, SEE YOU AGAIN--MAYBE!
Copyright 1939, McClure Newspaper Syndicate
I'VE ALWAYS DREAMED OF FINDING SO MASTERFUL A GALLANT! WE'LL MEET AGAIN...BUT NEXT TIME HE WON'T GET AWAY SO EASILY!
183

LATER -- SUPERMAN DROPS UPON THE LEDGE OF CLARK KENT'S APARTMENT...
NOW TO PHONE IN MY STORY!
184
Copyright 1939, McClure Newspaper Syndicate
CLARK KENT SPEAKING! CONNECT ME WITH A RE-WRITE MAN!
IN A DISTANT ROOM, PLOTTERS FUME ..
THE SUBMARINE WAS DESTROYED. AND THE KING AND PRINCESS LIVE!
WHAT NOW?
YES, WE'VE FAILED THIS TIME....
BUT ONLY TEMPORARILY! THE MILAN DOCKS TOMORROW MORNING ----NEXT TIME WE WON'T MISS!

NOW TO RETURN TO LOIS' APARTMENT! I'LL HAVE SOME JOB EXPLAINING MY ABSENCE!
AGAIN SUPERMAN DONS HIS GUISE OF CLARK KENT, ACE DAILY STAR REPORTER..
YOU--!
ER ---I GUESS IT IS!
185 Copyright 1939, McClure Newspaper Syndicate

WHAT'S THE IDEA OF RUNNING OUT ON A DATE, AFTER BEGGING FOR ONE FOR MONTHS?
IT'S VERY SIMPLE TO EXPLAIN. YOU SEE...I...
I'M NOT INTEREST-ED IN YOUR EXPLANATIONS! GET OUT!
IF YOU'D ONLY LET ME EXPLAIN!
AFTER CLARK DEPARTS, LOIS TAKES A WALK TO COOL OFF....
OF ALL THE SHABBY TRICKS!
EXTRA! SPECIAL DAILY STAR EXTRA!!
Copyright 1939, McClure Newspaper Syndicate
186
I'LL TAKE ONE, PLEASE!
HM-M!--I WONDER WHAT THEY'VE BROUGHT OUT AN EXTRA ABOUT?
DAILY

WELL, I'LL ---!
Daily Star
SUBMARINE ATTACKING ROYAL COUPLE DESTROYE AT SEA BY SUPERMAN!
by Clark Kent
BY CLARK! HOW COULD HE HAVE LEFT MY APARTMENT AND GATHERED THIS INFORMATION IN SUCH A SHORT TIME?
187
SO THE MILAN DOCKS TOMORROW MORNING AT 9:00 A.M., EH? -- I'LL BE THERE!
BOARD BUS HERE
SAND
Copyright 1939, McClure Newspaper Syndicate
EARLY NEXT MORNING...
WHY, LOIS --- WHAT ARE YOU DOING HERE?
MINDING MY OWN AFFAIRS, AND I'D BE OBLIGED IF YOU'D DO THE SAME!

MEANWHILE, IN A DISTANT OFFICE...
YOU WILL ALL DRAW SLIPS. TO THE FORTUNATE ONE WHO DRAWS THE MARKED SLIP WILL FALL THE ENVIABLE TASK OF ASSASSINATING THE KING AND PRINCESS!
188
I HAVE THE MARKED SLIP!
SPLENDID! GO NOW TO WHERE THE MILAN DOCKS, AND DO YOUR TASK WELL!
THE MILAN SWERVES IN TOWARD THE DOCK...
Copyright 1939, McClure Newspaper Syndicate
AS AN ODDLY ASSORTED CROWD ANXIOUSLY AWAITS ITS FIRST GLIMPSE OF ROYALTY ...CLARK, LOIS, THE PRESS, GOVERNMENT OFFICIALS, AND --- THE ASSASSIN!

WHY THE HEAVY GUARD, FATHER?
JUST A PRECAUTIONARY MEASURE!
Copyright 1939, McClure Newspaper Syndicate
AT THAT MOMENT...KENT'S TELESCOPIC VISION REVEALS TO HIM...
GOOD GRIEF!
...THE ASSASSIN...SLIPPING A DEADLY BOMB FROM UNDER HIS JACKET!
DEATH TO THE ROYAL HOUSE OF RANGORIA!
189
WHAT'LL I DO? HE'S TOO FAR FROM ME TO STOP HIM NATURALLY, AND IF I USE SUPER-STRENGTH, I WILL REVEAL MY IDENTITY AS SUPERMAN!

GIVE ME THAT!
HEY! WHAT ARE--?
CLARK HURLS THE CAMERA THRU THE AIR WITH GREAT FORCE!
STRAIGHT AND TRUE IT FLIES, STRIKING THE ASSASSIN DIRECTLY UPON HIS WRIST...!
OW-WW!
190
...DOWN FROM THE PIER DROPS THE BOMB, TO BE SWALLOWED BY THE OCEAN AND RENDERED HARMLESS!
Copyright 1939, McClure Newspaper Syndicate

GET HIM!
HE TRIED TO ASSASSINATE THE KING AND PRINCESS!
THE DIRTY KILLER!
NO--- DON'T..!
YOU'LL NEVER GET ME!
A GREAT WAVE RAMS THE PONDEROUS MILAN UP AGAINST THE DOCK...
--A SOUL-SHIVERING SHRIEK, THEN... SILENCE...
HE--HE WAS CRUSHED TO DEATH!
BUT HE DESERVED IT!
Copyright 1939, McClure Newspaper Syndicate 191

NICE GOIN', FELLA!
HE'S A HERO!
HEY! LET ME OUT!
LET ME SEE HIM!
CLARK--- A HERO! I--DON'T --GET --IT.
192
AT THE FIRST OPPORTUNITY, CLARK SLIPS AWAY...
WHEW! IF THAT'S HERO WORSHIP... I WANT NONE OF IT!
PIER-NO
Copyright 1939, McClure Newspaper Syndicate
HELLO, DAILY STAR? CONNECT ME WITH A REWRITE-MAN! HERE'S A STORY THAT'LL MAKE ANOTHER EXTRA!

NEXT MORNING... AS CLARK ENTERS THE DAILY STAR OFFICE...
HAIL TO THE HERO!
IS IT TRUE, CLARK-- THAT YOU SAVED THE KING AND QUEEN FROM ASSASSINATION?
WHOA!-- YOU TAKE MY BREATH AWAY!
HOW DID IT HAPPEN?
IT WAS REALLY AN ACCIDENT. YOU SEE...
SAY, CLARK! THERE'S A GUY WAITING TO SEE YOU--- MUST BE A BIG SHOT... HE'S LOADED DOWN WITH MEDALS!
KING BORU AND PRINCESS TANIA GRACIOUSLY EXTEND TO YOU AN INVITATION TO VISIT THEM AND RECEIVE THEIR ROYAL THANKS!
I'LL BE DELIGHTED TO ACCEPT!
193 Copyright 1939, McClure Newspaper Syndicate
WHATAMAN! HOBNOBBING WITH ROYALTY, AND EVERYTHING!
IT'S JUST IN THE BREAKS ... MIGHT HAVE HAPPENED TO ANY OF YOU!
--CLARK KENT--- THE CENTER OF ATTENTION... ACQUAINTED WITH ROYALTY!

AN INVITATION FROM THE KING AND PRINCESS OF RANGORIA! NOT BAD!
Copyright 1939, McClure Newspaper Syndicate
NO ONE IS PERMITTED TO ENTER
BUT--!
BUT I WAS INVITED TO COME. MY NAME IS CLARK K--
CLARK KENT!-- A THOUSAND PARDON'S!-- ENTER!
194
M-MM! SOME SHACK!

THIS PLACE CERTAINLY IS WELL-GUARDED!
Copyright 1939, McClure Newspaper Syndicate
IF YOU'LL BE SEATED, YOUR HOSTS WILL SOON JOIN YOU!
195
I WISH THEY'D HURRY. I FEEL LOST IN THE VASTNESS OF THIS ROOM!
KING BORU AND PRINCESS TANIA OF RANGORIA!

SO YOU'RE THE YOUNG MAN TO WHOM WE OWE OUR LIVES!
YOU HAVE OUR ROYAL GRATITUDE!
THANK YOU, YOUR HIGHNESS!
196
YOU SHALL BE REWARDED FOR YOUR BRAVERY!
NAME ANYTHING!
AN INTERVIEW WITH YOU WILL BE REWARD ENOUGH! YOU SEE, I'M A REPORTER!
AND SO CLARK'S REQUEST IS GRANTED...
WHOM DO I THINK RESPONSIBLE FOR THE SUBMARINE ATTACK?--MY GUESS IS THAT THE "BLACK GANG", A GROUP OF RANGORIAN TERRORISTS, IS TO BLAME!
THIS'LL MAKE FINE COPY!
Copyright 1939, McClure Newspaper Syndicate
AND NOW THAT THE INTERVIEW IS FINISHED... MAY I HAVE A FEW WORDS WITH YOU?
CERTAINLY. ("-HM-MM! WHAT NOW?-")

WHAT I'M GOING TO ASK YOU IS STRICTLY OFF THE RECORD!
YOU MAY RELY ON MY DISCRETION!
197
WHO IS THIS SUPERMAN, WHO RESCUED US FROM THE SUBMARINE'S ATTACK?
SUPERMAN!--ER-- HE'S A MAN POSSESSING SUPER-STRENGTH WHO BATTLES INJUSTICE AND ASSISTS THE OPPRESSED. VERY LITTLE IS KNOWN OF HIM
WHY DO YOU ASK?
BECAUSE I HAVE A TREMENDOUS INTEREST IN HIM!
Copyright 1939, McClure Newspaper Syndicate
197
IN FACT, I THINK I'VE FALLEN IN LOVE WITH HIM!
("--WHAT A SPOT TO BE IN! IF SHE SUSPECTED MY TRUE IDENTITY..!")

MORE THAN ANYTHING ELSE, I WANT TO MEET SUPERMAN AGAIN. YOU'LL HELP ME FIND HIM, WON'T YOU?
I'LL DO EVERYTHING I CAN.
BE SURE TO ATTEND THE RECEPTION BEING HELD HERE TONIGHT.--I'LL EXPECT YOU.
RECEPTION? --ER--I'LL BE THERE!
Copyright 1939, McClure Newspaper Syndicate
WITHIN THE NEXT ROOM, THE BUTLER SURREPTIOUSLY MAKES A PHONE CALL...
OPERATOR X-11, SPEAKING-- THE YOUNG REPORTER HAS JUST RECEIVED AN INVITATION TO THE RECEPTION BEING HELD HERE TONIGHT!
CLARK'S SUPER-HEARING ENABLES HIM TO HEAR THE CLICKING OF THE TELEPHONE'S DIAL-MECHANISM...
3--8-- 3425!
198

UPON LEAVING THE KING'S RESIDENCE, CLARK CALLS THE CHIEF OPERATOR...
KENT OF THE DAILY STAR SPEAKING! WILL YOU PLEASE GIVE ME THE NAME AND ADDRESS LISTED FOR 3-8-3425?
DR. LARRON-- 381 PARMALEE... THANK YOU, OPERATOR!
A BUTLER PHONES. A DOCTOR...INFORMS HIM OF MY VISIT--- BUT WHY?
I'LL DROP IN ON THIS DR. LARRON, AND LEARN THE ANSWER!
Copyright 1939, McClure Newspaper Syndicate
199

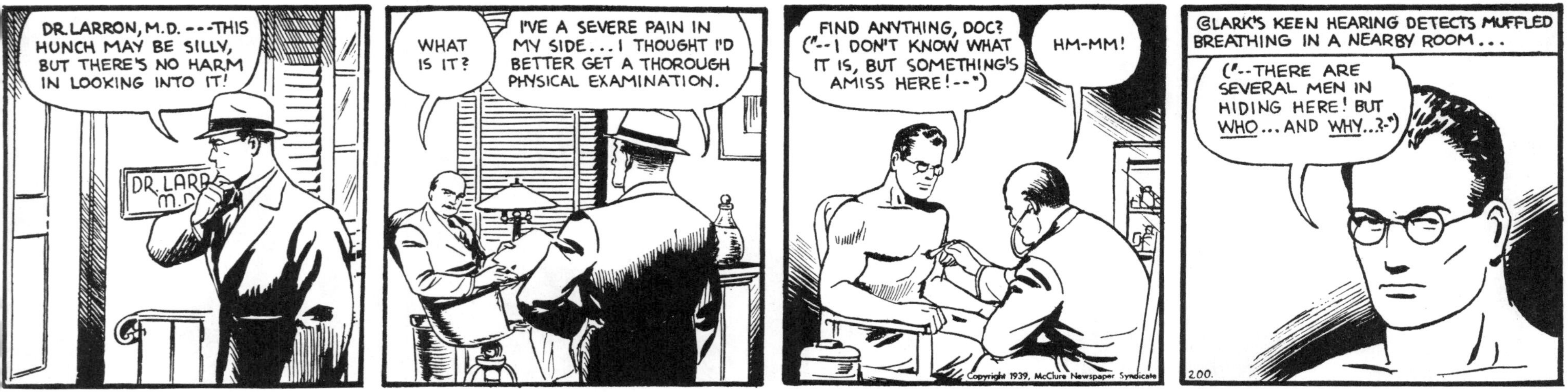
DR. LARRON, M.D. ---THIS HUNCH MAY BE SILLY, BUT THERE'S NO HARM IN LOOKING INTO IT!
DR. LARR
M.D
WHAT IS IT?
I'VE A SEVERE PAIN IN MY SIDE... I THOUGHT I'D BETTER GET A THOROUGH PHYSICAL EXAMINATION.
FIND ANYTHING, DOC? ("--I DON'T KNOW WHAT IT IS, BUT SOMETHING'S AMISS HERE!--")
HM-MM!
Copyright 1939, McClure Newspaper Syndicate
CLARK'S KEEN HEARING DETECTS MUFFLED BREATHING IN A NEARBY ROOM...
("--THERE ARE SEVERAL MEN IN HIDING HERE! BUT WHO... AND WHY..?-")
200.

WELL DOC! WHAT'S THE VERDICT?
THERE'S NOTHING WRONG WITH YOU. YOU'RE IN PERFECT PHYSICAL CONDITION.
IN THAT CASE I'LL PAY THE FEE, BE GLAD YOU FOUND NOTHING WRONG WITH ME, AND LEAVE.
OH, NO YOU WON'T! STAND WHERE YOU ARE!
201
YOU MAY ENTER NOW!
DON'T MOVE!
WHAT IN--?
WHAT DOES THIS MEAN?
DON'T ACT SO SURPRISED! WE KNOW WHO YOU ARE AND WE THINK WE KNOW WHY YOU'VE COME!
Copyright 1939, McClure Newspaper Syndicate

IS IT CUSTOMARY FOR YOU TO TREAT YOUR PATIENTS THIS WAY, DR. LARRON?
YOU'RE A REPORTER NAMED CLARK KENT AND YOU'VE COME STRAIGHT HERE FROM KING BORU'S RESI-DENCE! WHY?
AS CLARK, SILENT, SMILES...
I ADVISE YOU TO TALK!
YOU'D BETTER DO AS HE SAYS, IF YOU WANT TO REMAIN HEALTHY!
DON'T GRIN AT ME LIKE AN APE! START TALKING!
202
Copyright 1939, McClure Newspaper Syndicate
REFUSE TO SPEAK, EH?-- PERHAPS WE KNOW HOW TO LOOSEN YOUR TONGUE!

WHEN CLARK REFUSES TO OFFER INFORMATION, DR. LARRON PRODUCES A VISE . . .
YOU'LL BE TALKING SOON...BEGGING FOR MERCY!
THE PLOTTERS FORCE CLARK'S HAND WITHIN THE DEVICE . . .
Copyright 1939, McClure Newspaper Syndicate
YOUR LAST CHANCE! WILL YOU SPEAK, OR MUST WE BEGIN THIS UNPLEASANT DEMONSTRATION?
HE STILL REFUSES TO TALK!
203
YOU MAY BEGIN!

LEERING, ONE OF DR. LARRON'S HENCHMEN TIGHTENS THE VISE . . .
TALK...OR HAVE THE BONES OF YOUR HAND **SLOWLY CRUSHED!**
BUT CLARK'S ONLY REACTION TO THE TORTURE IS A MADDENING GRIN...
204
(PUFF!) I'M GIVING IT ALL I'VE GOT BUT (PUFF!) IT DOESN'T SEEM TO BOTHER HIM!
WHEW! HE CERTAINLY CAN TAKE IT!
Copyright 1939, McClure Newspaper Syndicate
UNDER THE HENCHMAN'S FRENZIED EFFORTS THE VISE BEGINS TO SLOWLY TWIST OUT OF SHAPE . . .
TURN! TURN!-- OUR SUPERIOR MUST BE INFORMED OF EVERYTHING THIS MAN KNOWS!
("-'SUPERIOR', EH? THEN THERE'S A MAN EVEN HIGHER UP, WHOM I MUST MEET! IT'S TIME I STOPPED PLAYING WITH THESE MEN AND DID SOMETHING!-")

THE VISE INTENDED TO CRUSH CLARK'S HAND SLOWLY BECOMES TWISTED...
("- I'VE GOT TO PLAY ALONG WITH THEM... PRETEND THIS HURTS, SO THAT I CAN LEARN THE IDENTITY OF THEIR LEADER!-")
205
I CAN'T STAND IT ANY LONGER! THE PAIN...! STOP! STOP!
I KNEW HE WOULD CRACK!
LISTEN TO ME! WE'LL PAY YOU MONEY--ONE HUNDRED THOUSAND DOLLARS--IF YOU WORK FOR US, DO AS WE SAY!
LET-- ME-- GO!
Copyright 1939, McClure Newspaper Syndicate
I'LL DO IT! I'LL DO ANYTHING YOU SAY!
THAT'S BETTER! --FREE HIM!

I OVERHEARD THE KING'S BUTLER TELEPHONE YOU AND CAME HERE ON THE TRACK OF A NEWS STORY.
I HOPE YOU ARE TELLING THE TRUTH. --BUT ANYHOW, WE CAN MAKE IMPORTANT USE OF YOU.
Copyright 1939, McClure Newspaper Syndicate
THE DOCTOR STRIDES ABOUT, LOST IN THOUGHT, THEN -- SUDDENLY....
I'VE GOT IT--A PLAN THAT I'M SURE OUR LEADER WILL APPROVE!
WHAT IS IT?
206
WHEN KENT ATTENDS THE RECEPTION TONIGHT, HE WILL GET THE PRINCESS TO GO RIDING WITH HIM ON SOME PRETEXT, THEN DRIVE TO AN AGREED SPOT.
THERE WE WILL KIDNAP HER. WITH PRINCESS TANIA IN OUR HANDS, HER FATHER, THE KING, WILL BE FORCED TO GIVE US THE CONCESSIONS WE DESIRE!
SPLENDID! A BRILLIANT PLAN!
NOT BAD AT THAT... ESPECIALLY FOR ME, WHEN I GET THAT HUNDRED THOUSAND DOLLARS!

IT'S AGREED THAT I LEAD THE PRINCESS TO A SPOT WHERE YOU WILL SEIZE HER. BUT WHAT HAPPENS THEN?
WE WILL TAKE HER TO OUR LEADER WHO WILL THEN DEMAND OF THE KING THE CONCESSIONS WE DESIRE.
AFTER CLARK DEPARTS...
QUIET! I'M CONTACTING THE LEADER!
MY PLAN IS TO KIDNAP THE PRINCESS WITH THE REPORTER'S ASSISTANCE, AND BRING HER TO YOU!
IT IS AN EXCELLENT PLAN!
207
HOWEVER, INSTEAD OF BRINGING PRINCESS TANIA TO ME, KILL HER!
WE WILL DO AS YOU DIRECT!
Copyright 1939, McClure Newspaper Syndicate

THAT EVENING---
THE BELL!- I WONDER WHO THAT IS?
Copyright 1939, McClure Newspaper Syndicate
LOIS!
YES...IT'S ME, ALL RIGHT!
208
BUT--BUT WHY THE UNEXPECTED VISIT?
YOU DON'T KNOW IT YET, CLARK, BUT I'M GOING TO THAT ROYAL RECEPTION WITH YOU!
THIS IS A PLEASURE I DIDN'T COUNT ON!
WELL, DON'T LET IT GIVE YOU ANY WRONG IDEAS. THE EDITOR ASSIGNED ME TO TAG ALONG WITH YOU. I ASSURE YOU, THIS IS PURELY A BUSINESS MATTER!

ARRIVING AT THE RECEPTION...
NOT A BAD PLACE, IS IT?
I STILL PREFER MY SMALL APARTMENT.
Copyright 1939, McClure Newspaper Syndicate
AS THEY ENTER THE BALLROOM, CLARK IS OVERWHELMED BY THE ACCLAMATION OF THE GUESTS....
SO YOU'RE THE HEROIC MAN WE'VE BEEN HEARING SO MUCH ABOUT!
GLAD TO MEET YOU SIR,-- GLAD!
YOU'VE DONE RANGORIA A SERVICE IT WILL NEVER FORGET!
THIS IS MY DANCE! REMEMBER? YOU PROMISED!
YOUR ATTENTION IS FLATTERING, PRINCESS!
WELL, DON'T BE TOO FLATTERED! I'M DANCING WITH YOU ONLY BECAUSE I WANT TO LEARN MORE ABOUT *SUPERMAN!*
ASK AWAY! ("--I'M AFRAID THIS IS GOING TO BE EMBARRASSING!--")
209

TELL ME, IS THERE ANY WAY ONE CAN CONTACT THIS--ER-- *SUPERMAN?*
IT WOULD BE VERY DIFFICULT INDEED. BUT POSSIBLE, PERHAPS...
HE MAKES ME FURIOUS! NOT THAT I'M JEALOUS, BUT HE COULD SHOW ME A LITTLE MORE ATTENTION.
210
WHEN THE DANCE ENDS...
SINCE YOU BROUGHT ME HERE, DON'T YOU THINK THAT YOU MIGHT DANCE WITH ME ONCE, FOR APPEARANCE'S SAKE?
GLADLY!--LET'S MAKE IT THE NEXT DANCE!
BUT I PROMISED LOIS I'D..
FORGET IT! YOU'RE COMING WITH ME!
Copyright 1939, McClure Newspaper Syndicate

ACCEDING TO THE PRINCESS'S REQUEST, CLARK TAKES HER FOR A SPIN THROUGH THE NIGHT...
Copyright 1939, McClure Newspaper Syndicate
("--EVERYTHING'S WORKING OUT AS THE PLOTTERS PLANNED, BUT I WONDER WHETHER IT'S SUCH A GOOD IDEA TO PRETEND TO FALL IN WITH THEM.--")
MIND IF WE PARK HERE?
NOT AT ALL
211
YOU KNOW, DESPITE MY FEELINGS FOR SUPERMAN, THERE'S SOMETHING ABOUT YOU THAT ATTRACTS ME, TOO.
ER--- REALLY?

THE PRINCESS PURSUES A DANGEROUS LINE OF QUESTIONING....
ODD --BUT WHEN THE SHADOWS FELL ACROSS YOUR FACE A MOMENT AGO, I WAS STARTLED BY YOUR RESEMBLANCE TO--SUPERMAN!
ME? --- RESEMBLE SUPERMAN?
BUT NOW THAT I LOOK CLOSER I CAN SEE THE FANCIED RESEMBLANCE WAS JUST A TRICK OF MY IMAGINATION!
("--HOW SILLY OF ME TO COMPARE THE TWO--SUPERMAN IS SO BOLD AND DARING ...WHILE THIS ANEMIC WRETCH IS AFRAID OF HIS OWN SHADOW!--")
("--WHEW! SHE HAD ME NERVOUS THERE, FOR A MOMENT!--")
212
ONTO THIS SCENE GLIDES THE RANGORIAN PLOTTERS' SLEEK, DARK SEDAN..
Copyright 1939, McClure Newspaper Syndicate

UP WITH YOUR HANDS AND GET OUT!
HUH?
YOU HEARD ME --OUT!
WHAT IN--?
213
THIS IS SO THAT YOU WON'T INTERFERE!
UH-HH-H!
TAKE YOUR HANDS OFF ME! LET ME GO!
QUICK! INTO THE CAR WITH HER BEFORE HE REVIVES!
Copyright 1939, McClure Newspaper Syndicate

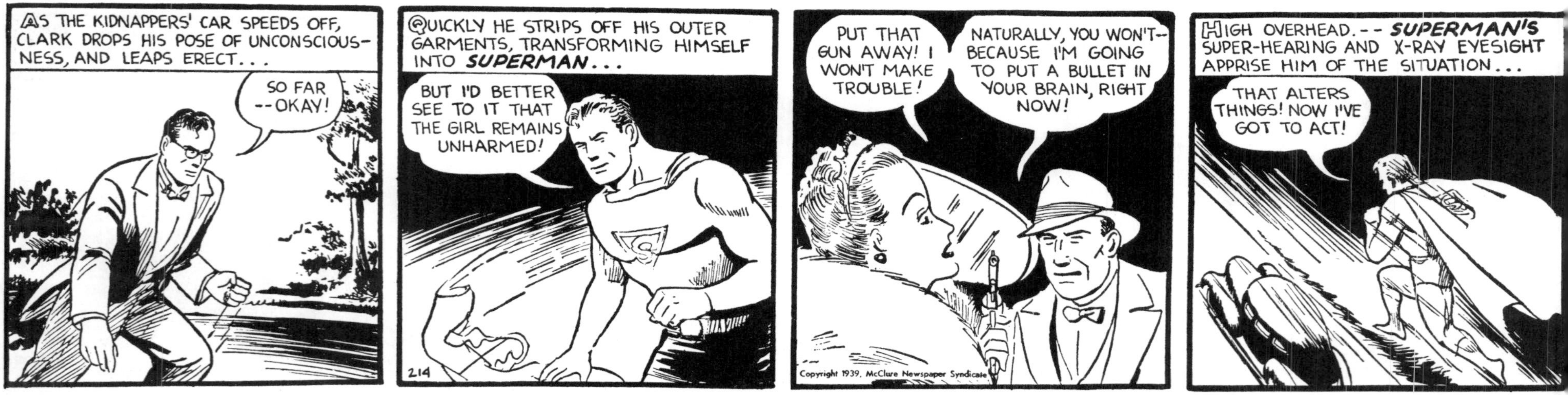
AS THE KIDNAPPERS' CAR SPEEDS OFF, CLARK DROPS HIS POSE OF UNCONSCIOUSNESS, AND LEAPS ERECT...
SO FAR --OKAY!
QUICKLY HE STRIPS OFF HIS OUTER GARMENTS, TRANSFORMING HIMSELF INTO SUPERMAN...
BUT I'D BETTER SEE TO IT THAT THE GIRL REMAINS UNHARMED!
214
PUT THAT GUN AWAY! I WON'T MAKE TROUBLE!
NATURALLY, YOU WON'T-- BECAUSE I'M GOING TO PUT A BULLET IN YOUR BRAIN, RIGHT NOW!
Copyright 1939, McClure Newspaper Syndicate
HIGH OVERHEAD.-- SUPERMAN'S SUPER-HEARING AND X-RAY EYESIGHT APPRISE HIM OF THE SITUATION...
THAT ALTERS THINGS! NOW I'VE GOT TO ACT!

215
WHAT IN--?
WHERE'D HE COME FROM?
Copyright 1939, McClure Newspaper Syndicate
AS THE AUTO SWERVES TO AVOID SUPERMAN'S FIGURE, THE HENCHMAN'S AIM IS DEFLECTED . . . .
WHAT--??
SWIFTER THAN LIGHTNING, SUPERMAN SEIZES AND TEARS OPEN THE REAR OF THE CAR!
STICK AROUND!

WITH A DEFT MOVEMENT HE REMOVES THE PRINCESS AS . . .
RUDELY, HE SPILLS OUT THE OCCUPANTS!
216
THEN, TO THEIR INCREDULOUS AMAZEMENT, SMASHES THE CAR TO BITS WITH ONE TERRIFIC BLOW OF HIS FIST...!
Copyright 1939, McClure Newspaper Syndicate

RUN FOR IT!
HE--- HE'S AFTER US!
Copyright 1939 McClure Newspaper Syndicate
HOLD ON!
YEEEE-EE!
IT'S BEEN A LONG TIME SINCE I'VE BOWLED, BUT-- HERE GOES!
217
AH-I HAVEN'T LOST MY FORM!

IF YOU MURDERING RATS WOULD LIKE A LITTLE MORE--!
NO! NO! ..WE'VE HAD ENOUGH!
LOOK! ANOTHER CAR!
FRIENDS! ---WE'RE SAVED!
FRIENDS, NOTHING! ---THOSE MACHINE-GUNS DON'T LOOK VERY AMICABLE!
218
THERE'S BEEN A SLIP UP! THE PRINCESS IS FREE!--SHOOT HER DOWN!
Copyright 1939, McClure Newspaper Syndicate
AT THE SOUND OF MACHINE-GUN FIRE, SUPERMAN SCOOPS UP THE PRINCESS AND LEAPS FOR THE TREE OVERHEAD...
IF YOU ONLY KNEW HOW I'VE LONGED TO HAVE YOU HOLD ME LIKE THIS--!
THIS IS NO TIME TO GET ROMANTIC!

SHOOT THEM DOWN!
219.
NOW, STAY HERE --- DON'T MOVE UNLESS I TELL YOU!
WE'RE TRAPPED! THEY'LL KILL US BOTH!
IF YOU'LL JUST STICK TO THIS SPOT, YOU WON'T GET HURT!
COME DOWN, OR WE'LL BLAST YOU DOWN!
COMING!
Copyright 1939, McClure Newspaper Syndicate

.220
GET HIM! RUN HIM DOWN!
Copyright 1939, McClure Newspaper Syndicate
LOOK OUT!

HEARING THE PRINCESS'S WARNING SHOUT SUPERMAN WRENCHES A TREE UP BY ITS ROOTS . . .
Copyright 1939, McClure Newspaper Syndicate
WHAM
221

HE RIPPED UP THE TREE--
--AND SMASHED IT INTO THE AUTO! HE'S GOT THE STRENGTH OF A THOUSAND MEN!
LET'S GET GOING!
222
OFF SOARS SUPERMAN, THE PRINCESS IN HIS ARMS, FOLLOWED BY MACHINE-GUN BURSTS . . .
Copyright 1939, McClure Newspaper Syndicate

TWO FIGURES RACE THRU THE SKY AT BREAKNECK SPEED... PRINCESS TANIA OF RANGORIA AND---SUPERMAN...
Copyright 1939, McClure Newspaper Syndicate
TRY NOT TO BE FRIGHTENED!
FRIGHTENED?-- I'M THRILLED!
223
YOU'RE SO STRONG AND I FEEL SO SAFE WITH YOU!
("—THERE SHE GOES AGAIN!—")
WHEN THEY REACH THE PRINCESS'S RESIDENCE...
DON'T LEAVE ME AGAIN. I'VE SOMETHING EXTREMELY IMPORTANT TO TELL YOU! WHEN I SIGNAL YOU FROM MY ROOM--COME!
I'LL AWAIT YOUR SIGNAL!

AT THE RECEPTION...
HAVE YOU SEEN THE PRINCESS?-- I'VE BEEN WONDERING WHERE SHE IS.
HERE COMES HER LADY-IN-WAITING, NOW.
THE PRINCESS IS VERY FATIGUED AND HAS RETIRED FOR THE EVENING.
POOR TANIA. SHE'S HAD A TRYING DAY.
224
CLARK AND THE PRINCESS HAVE BEEN GONE A MIGHTY LONG TIME. WHAT CAN THEY BE UP TO?
I WONDER WHAT THE PRINCESS WANTS TO TELL ME?
Copyright 1939, McClure Newspaper Syndicate

UPON REACHING HER ROOM, PRINCESS TANIA SWIFTLY CHANGES HER GARMENTS.
THIS NEGLIGEE SHOULD BE JUST THE THING!
IT'S CERTAINLY TAKING HER A LONG TIME TO REACH HER ROOM. I WONDER WHAT'S DELAYING HER?
Copyright 1939, McClure Newspaper Syndicate
THERE'S NOTHING LIKE THE DEVASTATING SCENT OF MIDNIGHT MADNESS TO REDUCE A MALE TO A QUIVERING SLAVE!
THE SIGNAL!
225

A LITHE SPRING BRINGS THE MAN OF STEEL TO THE PRINCESS'S BALCONY...
226
Copyright 1939, McClure Newspaper Syndicate
NO SIGN OF HER!
I'M SORRY IF I KEPT YOU WAITING!
WHAT DID YOU WISH TO SEE ME ABOUT?
CAN'T YOU GUESS?

I'VE NO TIME FOR RIDDLES. WHAT IS IT YOU WISH TO TELL ME?
ARE YOU SO BLIND THAT YOU CAN'T SEE I'M MAD ABOUT YOU?
YOU HAD ME COME UP HERE TO TELL ME THAT?
YES -- IT HAS BEEN YOUR GOOD FORTUNE TO ATTAIN THE LOVE OF A PRINCESS!
I'M VERY FLATTERED BY YOUR ATTENTION-- BUT I'M AFRAID YOU'VE MISPLACED YOUR AFFECTION.
WHAT...?
Copyright 1939, McClure Newspaper Syndicate
227

AM I TO UNDERSTAND THAT YOU ARE NOT INTERESTED IN MY DEVOTION? OTHERS HAVE FOUND ME IRRESISTIBLE!
PLEASE DON'T TAKE THIS AS A PERSONAL AFFRONT, BUT--
--MY LIFE IS DEVOTED TO BATTLING EVIL AND THERE IS NO PLACE IN MY SCHEME OF THINGS FOR ROMANCE!
Copyright 1939, McClure Newspaper Syndicate
YOU HAVE THE AUDACITY TO SPURN ME!
TO PUT IT BRIEFLY: YES!
228
SNATCHING UP A DAGGER, TANIA STRIKES AT SUPERMAN....
YOU--YOU BEAST...!

ENRAGED AT SUPERMAN'S INDIFFERENCE, PRINCESS TANIA STABS HIM....
TAKE THAT, YOU BEAST!
CAREFUL, THERE!
YOU MIGHT HURT YOURSELF!
OF COURSE--YOU'RE NOT HURT! I'D FORGOTTEN SUPERMAN WAS INVULNERABLE...!
Copyright 1939, McClure Newspaper Syndicate
LET GO OF ME! WHAT ARE YOU GOING TO DO?
229
GIVE YOU WHAT YOU DESERVE!

YOU CAN'T DO THIS TO ME.. A PRINCESS OF RANGORIA...
BUT I AM!
GET OUT!
GLADLY!
Copyright 1939, McClure Newspaper Syndica
I'D RATHER TACKLE A DINOSAUR THAN A WOMAN, ANYTIME!
230
I SHOULD HATE HIM---BUT I DON'T. I LOVE HIM!

DOWN TO EARTH STREAKS A FANTASTICALLY COSTUMED FIGURE . . .
IT'S TIME FOR CLARK KENT TO STEP BACK INTO THE PICTURE!
Copyright 1939, McClure Newspaper Syndicate
231
CLARK RETURNS TO THE ROYAL RECEPTION.
WHAT A TIME I'LL HAVE EXPLAINING TO LOIS!
I'D LIKE A WORD WITH YOU MR. KENT!
--ER--I'VE BEEN LOOKING FOR YOU!

SO YOU'VE FINALLY RETURNED!
LOIS! --ER-- I CAN EXPLAIN EVERYTHING!
Copyright 1939, McClure Newspaper Syndicate
PLEASE DANCE WITH ME SO THAT I CAN TELL YOU THE REASON FOR MY DISAPPEARANCE!
I'M NOT INTERESTED IN DANCING WITH YOU -- PLEASE TAKE ME HOME!
232
AS THEY DRIVE HOMEWARD, A COLD, BRITTLE SILENCE ENVELOPS THE TWO . . . .
SLAM!!
G-GOOD NIGHT!

NEXT MORNING... AS CLARK ENTERS THE DAILY STAR BUILDING . . .
PS-ST!
WHAT'S UP?
Copyright 1939, McClure Newspaper Syndicate
COME WITH ME! DR. LARRON WISHES TO SEE YOU AT ONCE!
LET'S GO!
LOIS, PASSING BY, OVERHEARS THEIR CONVERSATION . . .
WHAT WOULD THAT FOREIGN-LOOKING MAN WANT WITH CLARK?
REPORTORIAL AND FEMININE INSTINCTS PROMPT LOIS TO TRAIL THE ODD COUPLE..
IF THERE'S A STORY IN THE WIND, CLARK'S NOT GOING TO KEEP IT TO HIMSELF IF I CAN HELP IT!
TAX
233

WHEN CLARK AND HIS COMPANION REACH DR. LARRON'S OFFICE . . . .
WHAT'S UP?
YOU'RE JUST IN TIME FOR A COUNCIL OF WAR!
LARRON M.D.
234
FOR SOME REASON I CAN'T FATHOM, SUPERMAN SAVED THE PRINCESS FROM DEATH. -- IT'S APPARENT THAT AS LONG AS HE LIVES OUR PLANS ARE MENACED.
Copyright 1939, McClure Newspaper Syndicate
OUR LEADER HAS PREPARED A TRAP FOR SUPERMAN AT THE KENYON WAREHOUSE. -- IF WE COULD ONLY LURE HIM THERE...
PERHAPS I CAN BE OF ASSISTANCE.
TO THINK THAT CLARK WOULD BE A PARTY TO SUCH A DESPICABLE PLAN! I'M GLAD I TRAILED HIM! IT WILL BE A PLEASURE FOR ME TO EXPOSE HIM!
DR. LARRON M.D.

LOIS, OVERHEARING CLARK'S CONSENT TO TRAP SUPERMAN, DROPS HER POCKETBOOK IN THE SHOCK OF HER ANGER
OHH-HH!
Copyright 1939, McClure Newspaper Syndicate
A GIRL!
SEIZE HER!
LET ME GO!
235
LOIS! WHAT ARE YOU DOING HERE?
YOU KNOW HER? IF YOU'RE TRYING TO PULL ANYTHING...!*

WHO IS THIS GIRL?
A REPORTER ON MY PAPER... SHE MUST HAVE TRAILED ME HERE!
I NEVER DID LIKE YOU...AND NOW I SEE THAT MY INSTINCTIVE DISLIKE FOR YOU WAS WELL FOUNDED!
WELL, I KNOW HOW TO DEAL WITH CURIOUS WOMEN!
WAIT!
HOW DARE YOU INTERFERE?
DON'T SHOOT HER! KIDNAP HER! SUPERMAN HAS RESCUED HER BEFORE! HE MAY BE LURED TO THE WAREHOUSE BY THIS STRATEGY!
236
A SPLENDID SUGGESTION!
YOU--- YOU FILTHY TRAITOR!
Copyright 1939, McClure Newspaper Syndicate

AT KING BORU'S RESIDENCE, BREAKFAST IS BEING SERVED....
GOOD MORNING, YOUR MAGESTY.
GOOD MORNING!
UNSEEN BY THE ROYAL COUPLE, THE TRAITOROUS SERVANT DROPS A DRUG INTO THEIR COFFEE!...
237
SHORTLY AFTER...
I--I'M GETTING DIZZY!
FATHER--!
HURRY! OUT THE BACK WAY WITH THEM!
WE MUST ACT QUICKLY OR OUR LIVES WILL BE FORFEIT!
Copyright 1939, McClure Newspaper Syndicate

THE UNCONSCIOUS FIGURES OF THE KING AND PRINCESS OF RANGORIA ARE PLACED WITHIN A CAR AT THE REAR OF THEIR RESIDENCE....
Copyright 1939, McClure Newspaper Syndicate
AND A FEW MINUTES LATER, THE AUTO DRIVES OFF SWIFTLY WITH ITS ROYAL CAPTIVES!
WITHIN DR. LARRON'S OFFICE....
YOU PRINT THE STORY OF THE GIRL'S KIDNAPPING AS A BAIT FOR SUPERMAN!
I'VE A HUNCH THAT'LL DO THE TRICK!
238
COME ALONG, GIRLIE!

HOW CAN YOU STAND BY AND LET THEM GET AWAY WITH THIS?
YOU FORGET THAT I'M ONE OF THEM!
Copyright 1939, McClure Newspaper Syndicate
TOO BAD, LOIS, BUT MY HANDS ARE TIED . . . FOR THE PRESENT!
239
SWIFTLY, CLARK LOCATES A PUBLIC TELEPHONE . . . .
DAILY STAR? CLARK KENT SPEAKING. LOIS LANE HAS BEEN KIDNAPPED! I'M OFF TO FOLLOW A CLUE!
LATER--CLAD IN SUPERMAN UNIFORM...
NO TIME TO LOSE! LOIS NEEDS ME!

AS THE CONSPIRATORS' CAR DRAWS UP BEFORE THE KENYON WAREHOUSE, LOIS IS HUSTLED WITHIN THE BUILDING . . . .
WHAT ARE YOU DOING HERE?
I'M A CAPTIVE LIKE YOURSELF!
DON'T BE FRIGHTENED. I'M SURE THAT SUPERMAN WILL COME TO OUR RESCUE AGAIN, AND WHEN HE DOES . . .
AND WHEN HE DOES, I WILL BE DELIGHTED TO GREET HIM! I HAVE AN UNPLEASANT SURPRISE FOR THE MAN OF STEEL!
SUPERMAN IS STREAKING DOWN TOWARD THE WAREHOUSE AT THAT VERY MOMENT . . . .
I WONDER WHAT SORT OF A RECEPTION THEY'VE PREPARED FOR ME?
240
Copyright 1939, McClure Newspaper Syndicate

KOBER!-HOW DARE YOU CON-SPIRE AGAINST YOUR KING? I COMMAND...
YOU FORGET THAT I AM NOW IN THE POSITION TO ISSUE COMMANDS, YOUR MAJESTY! THERE ARE CERTAIN PAPERS I'D LIKE YOU TO SIGN!
HE'LL NEVER SIGN THEM! SUPER-MAN WILL HELP US!
I SHALL ATTEND TO THIS FANTASTIC SUPERMAN WHO HAS BEFRIENDED YOU. IT'S OBVIOUS I'M NO MATCH FOR HIM PHYSICALLY, AND SO...
241
I AM PREPARED FOR HIM! BEHOLD! GIANT WHIRLING MIRRORS TO RENDER HIM HELPLESS THROUGH HYPNOTISM!
YOU WON'T SUCCEED!
WON'T I? PERHAPS A PRACTICAL DEMONSTRATION WILL CHANGE YOUR MIND!
Copyright 1939, McClure Newspaper Syndicate

TO DEMONSTRATE THE POWER OF HIS HYPNOTIC MACHINE, KOBER TRAINS HIS MIRRORS ON LOIS, PULLS A SWITCH...
WATCH HER CLOSELY!
DON'T HARM THAT GIRL!
...BLINDING LIGHTS BLAZE DOWN AT LOIS, TRANSFIXING HER!
YOU SEE? SHE IS RIGID...HELP-LESS...SUBJECT TO MY EVERY WHIM!
YOU--- MONSTER...!
AND NOW...I RELEASE HER FROM HER TRANCE!
W-WHAT HAPPENED!
HE HYPNOTIZED YOU...WITH THAT TERRIBLE MACHINE!
WHILE OUTSIDE SUPERMAN ALIGHTS..
242 Copyright 1939, McClure Newspaper Syndicate

ACCORDING TO THIS PHOTO-ELECTRIC EYE SIGNAL, YOUR WOULD-BE RESCUER HAS JUST ALIGHTED UPON THE ROOF! IN A FEW MOMENTS YOU WILL SEE HOW POWERLESS HIS STEELY MUSCLES ARE AGAINST MY SUPERIOR MIND!
FINDING THE SKYLIGHT LOCKED, SUPERMAN RIPS IT OPEN....
SOMEWHERE IN THIS BUILDING LOIS IS HELD CAPTIVE! I MUST GET TO HER QUICKLY!
243
...DROPPING DOWN INTO A HALL....
Copyright 1939, McClure Newspaper Syndicate
HE CAUTIOUSLY MAKES HIS WAY ALONG IT UNTIL...
VOICES--ON THE OTHER SIDE OF THE WALL!

HEARING VOICES ON THE OTHER SIDE OF THE WALL, SUPERMAN GOES INTO ACTION....
HERE GOES!
Copyright
244
YOU'VE MET YOUR MATCH, SUPERMAN!
INSTANTLY, SEARING LIGHT-BEAMS FLASH FROM THE WHIRLING MIRRORS, BOMBARDING THE MAN OF STEEL!

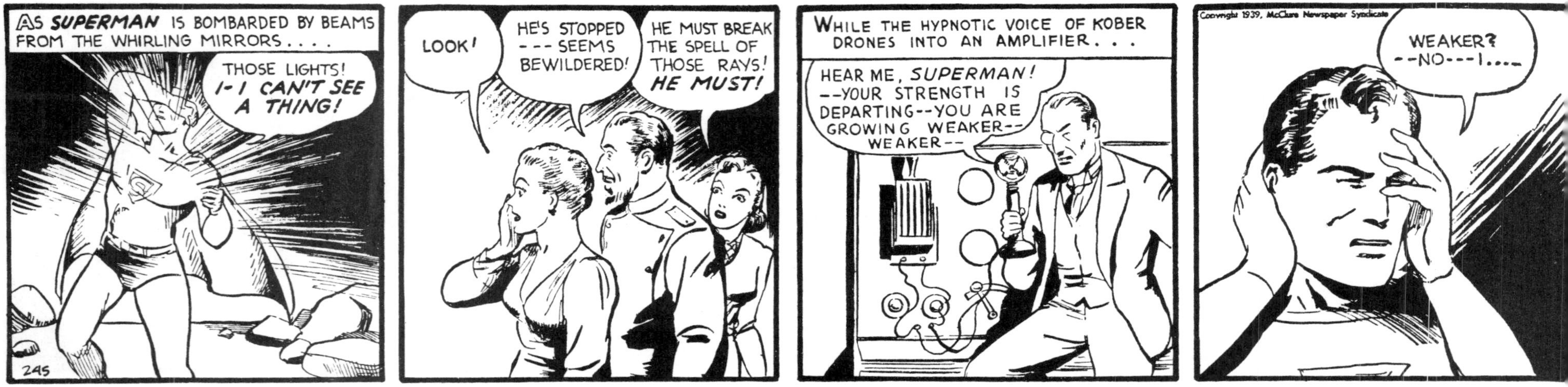
AS SUPERMAN IS BOMBARDED BY BEAMS FROM THE WHIRLING MIRRORS . . . .
THOSE LIGHTS! I-I CAN'T SEE A THING!
245
LOOK!
HE'S STOPPED --- SEEMS BEWILDERED!
HE MUST BREAK THE SPELL OF THOSE RAYS! HE MUST!
WHILE THE HYPNOTIC VOICE OF KOBER DRONES INTO AN AMPLIFIER . . .
HEAR ME, SUPERMAN! --YOUR STRENGTH IS DEPARTING--YOU ARE GROWING WEAKER-- WEAKER--
Copyright 1939, McClure Newspaper Syndicate
WEAKER? --NO---I....

SUMMONING ALL HIS WILL-POWER, SUPERMAN WAGES ONE OF THE STRANGEST BATTLES THE WORLD HAS YET SEEN! SUPER-STRENGTH PITTED AGAINST THE POWER OF HYPNOTISM-PLUS!
Copyright 1939, McClure Newspaper Syndicate
HE'S FIGHTING HIS WAY TOWARD KOBER --STEP BY STEP!
DON'T YIELD, SUPERMAN! YOU'RE GAINING!
246
NO MAN HAS SUFFICIENT WILL-POWER TO WITHSTAND THIS MACHINE! HE MUST FALTER ---HE MUST!

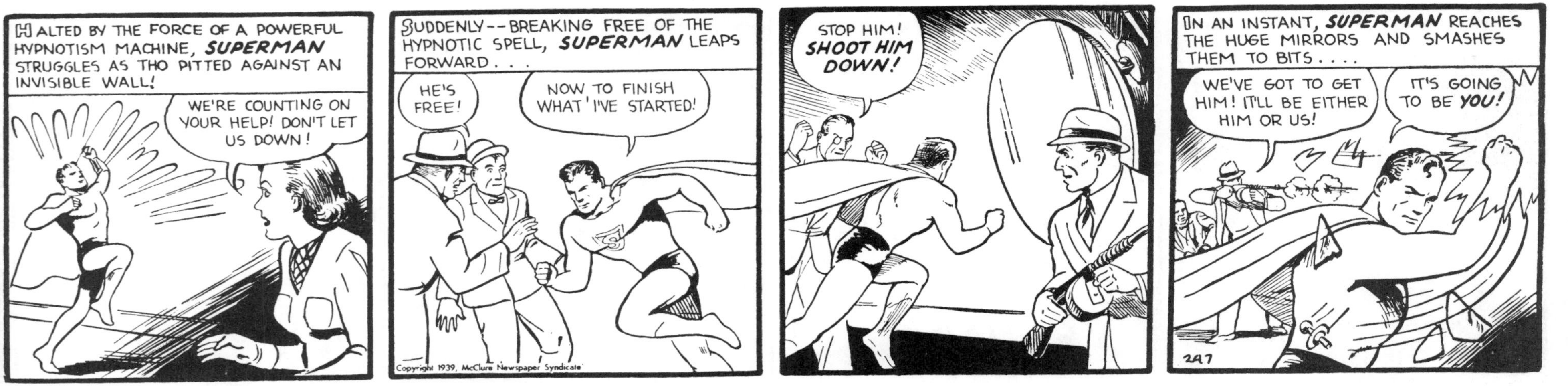
HALTED BY THE FORCE OF A POWERFUL HYPNOTISM MACHINE, SUPERMAN STRUGGLES AS THO PITTED AGAINST AN INVISIBLE WALL!
WE'RE COUNTING ON YOUR HELP! DON'T LET US DOWN!
SUDDENLY--BREAKING FREE OF THE HYPNOTIC SPELL, SUPERMAN LEAPS FORWARD . . .
HE'S FREE!
NOW TO FINISH WHAT I'VE STARTED!
Copyright 1939, McClure Newspaper Syndicate
STOP HIM! SHOOT HIM DOWN!
IN AN INSTANT, SUPERMAN REACHES THE HUGE MIRRORS AND SMASHES THEM TO BITS . . . .
WE'VE GOT TO GET HIM! IT'LL BE EITHER HIM OR US!
IT'S GOING TO BE YOU!
247

THE TERRIFIED PLOTTERS FLEE BEFORE SUPERMAN'S RUSH . . . .
STOP HIM, SOMEBODY!
YOU- STOP HIM!
DON'T ARGUE, BOYS! I'LL STOP YOU BOTH!
Copyright 1939, McClure Newspaper Syndicate
--LIKE THIS!
248
GET THRU THAT PANEL, QUICK!
I WON'T GO!
DON'T DELAY, OR HE'LL SHOOT YOU DOWN!
AS SUPERMAN SPRINGS TOWARD THE DEPARTING FIGURES, THE WALL PANEL SPRINGS SHUT!
TCH! TCH! --SUCH POOR MANNERS!

FASTER, FASTER! I'LL SHOOT THE FIRST ONE WHO LAGS BEHIND!
MOMENTARILY DELAYED BY A CLOSED PANEL, SUPERMAN HURLS HIMSELF AT IT..
IF HE THINKS HE'S GOING TO GET AWAY...
249
...HE'S GOT ANOTHER GUESS COMING!
FORWARD STREAKS SUPERMAN! --- SECONDS LATER, HE SIGHTS THOSE HE SEEKS!
IT WON'T BE LONG, NOW!
Copyright 1939, McClure Newspaper Syndicate

AS SUPERMAN APPROACHES, KOBER FORCES HIS CAPTIVES INTO A METAL-LINED ROOM...
HE'LL NEVER GET ME! I FORESAW THIS POSSIBILITY!
NOW TO SQUARE ACCOUNTS WITH YOU!
STAND BACK-- OR I'LL PULL THIS SWITCH!
Copyright 1939, McClure Newspaper Syndicate
THIS SWITCH CAN KILL US ALL! THIS ROOM IS ELECTRICALLY LINED. THE MOMENT THE CONNECTION IS MADE, WE'LL ALL BE ELECTROCUTED!
250
DOWN DESCENDS THE SWITCH!

AS KOBER JERKS THE SWITCH THREATENING ELECTROCUTION TO ALL...
A MATTER OF SECONDS!
251
Copyright 1939, McClure Newspaper Syndicate
AS HIS HANDS ENCOUNTER THE SWITCH, SUPERMAN RIPS IT CLEAR OFF THE WALL!
AND THAT--IS THAT!

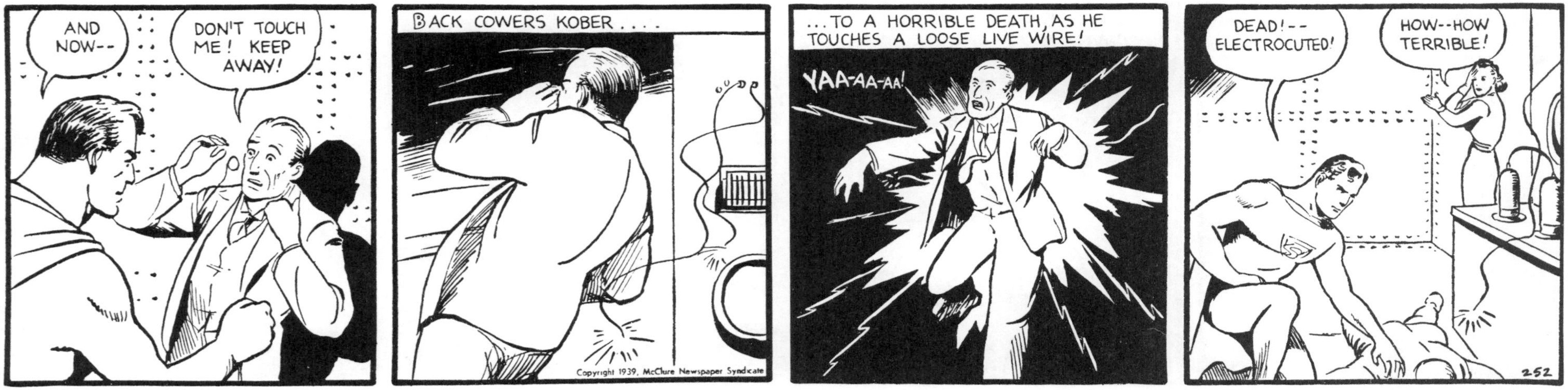
AND NOW--
DON'T TOUCH ME! KEEP AWAY!
BACK COWERS KOBER....
Copyright 1939, McClure Newspaper Syndicate
...TO A HORRIBLE DEATH, AS HE TOUCHES A LOOSE LIVE WIRE!
YAA-AA-AA!
DEAD!--ELECTROCUTED!
HOW--HOW TERRIBLE!
252

YOU HAVE THE GRATITUDE OF A KING!
ONLY TOO GLAD TO HELP OUT A PAL, BORU!
Copyright 1939, McClure Newspaper Syndicate
YOU *WONDERFUL* MAN!
I'M SO HAPPY I COULD KISS YOU... I *WILL* KISS YOU!
WHAT'S GOING ON HERE?
THE POLICE!
HELLO, CAPTAIN! THIS IS ONE TIME I'M CERTAINLY GLAD TO SEE YOU.
BEGORRA! I'VE DONE IT!...I'VE CAPTURED *SUPERMAN!*
MY CONGRATULATIONS, CAPTAIN.
253

SO I'VE CAPTURED THE FAMOUS *SUPERMAN!* THIS IS GOIN' TO BE QUITE A FEATHER IN MY CAP!
I HATE TO DISAPPOINT YOU, CAPTAIN, BUT--
...CAPTURING ME, AND *HOLDING* ME, ARE TWO DIFFERENT THINGS!
STOP HIM! HE MUSN'T GET AWAY!
254
A CHASE ENSUES, UNTIL...
THERE HE GOES! AN' I ALMOST HAD MY HANDS ON HIM!
THE COMMISSIONER WILL BE DISAPPOINTED. HE WANTS TO KNOW THAT GUY BETTER!
WHAT A MAN! —THEY DON'T COME LIKE THAT IN *RANGORIA!*
AND THEY DON'T COME LIKE THAT HERE EITHER.
Copyright 1939, McClure Newspaper Syndicate

HOLD ON! WHERE DO YOU THINK YOU'RE GOING?
I'M A REPORTER ...MUST TURN IN THIS STORY!
SORRY, BUT YOU'LL ALL HAVE TO COME ALONG TO THE STATION!
BUT I TELL YOU I'M THE KING OF RAN-GORIA!
YEAH?-AN' I'M LITTLE LORD FAUNT-LEROY'S LONG LOST BROTHER!
LATER--AT A PRECINCT STATION..
MY HUMBLE APOLOGIES, YOUR MAJESTY. OF COURSE, YOU'RE FREE TO GO!
THANKS, SARGE!
Copyright 1939, McClure Newspaper Syndicate
HAVE I A STORY! THIS OUGHT TO GET ME OFF THE LOVE-LORN ASSIGNMENT AND INTO THE NEWS COLUMNS!
OUT OF MY WAY, YOU ORDINARY MORTALS! I'VE JUST UNCOVERED A YARN THAT'LL MAKE HISTORY! WHERE'S THE CHIEF?
IN HIS OFFICE, WONDERING WHERE YOU'VE BEEN!
255

A FRONT PAGE SCOOP --! --AND I'M GOING TO HAND IT TO YOU ON A PLATTER!
MAKE SENSE!
IT'S STARTLING NEWS! YOU WON'T BELIEVE YOUR EARS! FIRST--CLARK KENT IS A TRAITOR WHO WORKS HAND IN GLOVE WITH KIDNAPPERS AND MURDERERS, AND...
Copyright 1939, McClure Newspaper Syndicate
SOMEONE MENTION MY NAME?
256
CLARK KENT!--YOU DARE TO SHOW YOUR FACE AROUND HERE! YOU SCOUNDREL!

257
DON'T TRY TO DENY THAT YOU WORKED WITH THOSE KILLERS. YOU...
BEFORE YOU SAY ANY MORE, READ *THIS EXTRA!*
Copyright 1939, McClure Newspaper Syndicate
YOU'VE SCOOPED ME ON THE STORY! EXPOSED THE RANGORIAN PLOTTERS!
YOU SEE, LOIS--CLARK *PRETENDED* TO WORK WITH THOSE MEN SO THAT HE COULD GET THE MATERIAL FOR THIS EXPOSÉ! IT WAS HIS TIP-OFF THAT SENT THE POLICE TO THE WAREHOUSE.
I--- I SEE.
PLEASE FORGIVE ME. I--I'VE BEEN A FOOL!
AREN'T WE ALL---AT TIMES?

SEVERAL DAYS LATER . . .
I REGRET THAT WE MUST RE-TURN TO RAN-GORIA SO QUICKLY, BUT CONDITIONS MAKE IT IMPERATIVE!
I'LL ALWAYS REMEMBER YOU GAVE ME MY BIGGEST SCOOP!
AND WHAT DO YOU THINK OF THE HATS AMERICAN WOMEN WEAR?
THEY'RE ODD-BUT I ADORE THEM.
258
YOU'RE BOTH COR-DIALLY INVITED TO VISIT RANGORIA AS MY GUESTS, ANY TIME YOU PLEASE!
THANKS, YOUR HIGHNESS!
WE MAY TAKE YOU UP!
PLEASE DO!
I WISH WITH ALL MY HEART THAT SOMEDAY, SOMEWHERE, I WILL ENCOUNTER *SUPERMAN* AGAIN.
PERHAPS YOU WILL...WHO KNOWS?
AND AS THE ROYAL YACHT BEGINS ITS RETURN JOURNEY . . . . .
YOU KNOW, I HATE TO SEE THEM GO, THEY MIGHT HAVE BEEN A ROYAL COUPLE, BUT . . .
--THEY WERE TOPS!
Copyright 1939, McClure Newspaper Syndicate

EPISODE NINE
UNDERWORLD POLITICS

Superman—By Jerry Siegel and Joe Shuster

War on Crime

(Copyright, 1939.)

EDITORIAL OFFICE OF THE *DAILY PLANET*. . . . CLARK KENT, ACE REPORTER, GETS A RUSH ASSIGNMENT.
GET DOWN TO COUNTY JAIL AT ONCE! THINGS ARE ABOUT TO POP!
I'M PRACTICALLY THERE!
259
SHORTLY AFTER . . .
WHAT'S ALL THE EXCITEMENT, OFFICER?
D.A.'S ORDERS, ALL KNOWN CRIMINALS ARE BEING ROUNDED UP!
THE PRESS INTERVIEWS DISTRICT-ATTORNEY LAKE . . .
WHY THE WHOLESALE ARRESTS?
YEAH-- HOW COME?
DURING MY ELECTION CAMPAIGN, I SWORE TO RID *METROPOLIS* OF CRIMINALS. THIS IS MY FIRST MOVE!
MR. HENNESSY TO SEE YOU, MR. LAKE.
"D.A. INITIATES WAR ON CROOKS-'BIG MIKE' HENNESSY, POLITICAL BOSS, PAYS A VISIT. INTERESTING!"
GET ALONG BOYS...I'VE BEEN EXPECTING MR. HENNESSY!

Superman—By Jerry Siegel and Joe Shuster

Clark Wins a Bet

(Copyright, 1939.)

AS MIKE HENNESSEY, POLITICAL BOSS, CALLS ON DISTRICT ATTORNEY LAKE.
HAVE YOU GONE CRAZY--ARRESTING ALL THOSE MEN? I TELL YOU I DON'T LIKE IT!
SORRY, BUT THERE WILL BE NO MORE CODDLING OF CRIMINALS -- I MEAN BUSINESS!
THINK LAKE WILL CAPITULATE TO "BIG MIKE'S" POLITICAL PRESSURE?
"BIG MIKE" IS A TOUGH HOMBRE -HE ALWAYS GETS WHAT HE GOES AFTER!
BUT HE MAY HAVE MET HIS MATCH IN LAKE!
OH YEAH? A FIVE SPOT SAYS "BIG MIKE" WALKS OUT WITH THE D.A. EATIN' OUT OF HIS HAND.
I'LL TAKE THAT BET!
AND WHY NOT? CLARK'S SUPER-ACUTE HEARING HAS ENABLED HIM TO OVERHEAR THE TALK WITHIN...
GET THIS, LAKE! I RUN THIS TOWN! PLAY BALL WITH ME --RELEASE THOSE MEN--OR-I'LL BREAK YOU!
YOU'VE SAID ENOUGH. GET OUT!
260.
PAY UP!

Superman—By Jerry Siegel and Joe Shuster *A Signal* (Copyright, 1939.)

"BIG MIKE" HENNESSEY, CORRUPT POLITICIAN, HAS JUST BEEN TOSSED OUT BY THE NEW DISTRICT ATTORNEY WHOM HE HAD ATTEMPTED TO INTIMIDATE.
PLAYING GAMES, "BIG MIKE"?
WHAT A STORY! "POLITICAL BOSS AND DISTRICT ATTORNEY ENGAGE IN WRESTLING MATCH"!
SMILE, HENNESSEY!
IF YOU PRINT THIS, I'LL-I'LL...
("-HE JERKED HIS THUMB, AND THAT TOUGH LOOKING HANGER-ON NODDED AS THOUGH HE'D RECEIVED A SECRET SIGNAL! AM I JUST IMAGINING THINGS, OR . . ?")
ONE SIDE, YOU GUYS! I GOTTA APPOINTMENT WID TH' D.A., SEE?
YOU NEEDN'T SHOVE!
"AND NOW HE'S CALLING ON LAKE! I WONDER IF...?"
CLARK'S WORST SUSPICIONS ARE CONFIRMED WHEN HIS X-RAY VISION REVEALS, WITHIN THE THUG'S POCKET... A GUN!
Copyright 1939, McClure Newspaper Syndicate

Superman—By Jerry Siegel and Joe Shuster *Prepared for Action.* (Copyright, 1939.)

SO LONG, FELLOWS! NO NEED TO STICK AROUND ANY LONGER.
WHAT'S YOUR HURRY? SOMETHING NEW MIGHT TURN UP.
LET HIM GO, BEFORE I LOSE MY SHIRT TO HIM!
262.
IN A DESERTED ALLEY BESIDE CITY HALL, CLARK REMOVES HIS OUTER GARMENTS, TRANSFORMING HIMSELF INTO THE DYNAMIC SUPERMAN!
NEXT INSTANT, HE LAUNCHES HIMSELF UPWARD, PARALLEL TO THE BUILDING, IN A TERRIFIC LEAP. . .
LEAPING SKYSCRAPERS, RACING TRAINS, SPRINGING GREAT HEIGHTS AND DISTANCES, LIFTING AND SMASHING PONDEROUS WEIGHTS, POSSESSING AN IMPENETRABLE SKIN- SUPERMAN USES THESE AMAZING ATTRIBUTES TO ASSIST THE OPPRESSED AND BATTLE INJUSTICE!

Superman—By Jerry Siegel and Joe Shuster *An Impertinent Query.* (Copyright, 1939.)

MEANWHILE IN THE DISTRICT-ATTORNEY'S OFFICE . . .
.. AND WHAT CAN I DO FOR YOU?
I GOTTA LITTLE BUSINESS T' TRANSACT WID YA!
"FINGER" McGURK'S MY NAME! HEARD OF ME?
YES, YOU'RE ONE OF THE HOODLUMS WHO ESCAPED THE ROUNDUP. BUT I CAN REMEDY THAT...
PUT DOWN THAT PHONE! YOU AN' ME IS GONNA HAVE A PRIVATE TALK!
YOU CAN'T GET AWAY WITH THIS!
THERE'S A MATTER O' SOME PALS OF MINE YA' LOCKED UP. WILL YA' FREE 'EM, OR. . .?
YOU DON'T FRIGHTEN ME, McGURK!
263
TOO BAD, MR. LAW. . . FER YOU!
DID ANYONE EVER INFORM YOU, "FINGER", THAT YOU RESEMBLE A RODENT?

Superman—By Jerry Siegel and Joe Shuster *Superman Acquiesces* (Copyright, 1939.)

A VOICE FROM BEHIND STARTLES "FINGER" McGURK . . . . . .
WH-WHAT'S THAT?
YOU HEARD ME. I SAID THAT THERE'S SOMETHING EXTREMELY DISAGREEABLE ABOUT YOUR FACE.
H-HOW DID YOU GET HERE?
I'LL GIVE YOU THREE GUESSES.
WHO'S THAT GUY AN' HOW'D HE GET IN HERE?
NEVER MET THE GENTLEMAN BEFORE.
DON'T YOU THINK IT'S ABOUT TIME YOU LOWERED THAT GUN, "FINGER"?
264
I DON'T KNOW WHO YA ARE-AN' I DON'T CARE. BUT YA STUCK YOUR NOSE INTO THE WRONG SPOT-AN' THAT'S JUST TOO BAD FER YA! GET OVER BESIDE LAKE!
YOU'D BETTER DO AS HE SAYS.
I SUPPOSE I'D BETTER.

uperman—By Jerry Siegel and Joe Shuster *Superman Grins* (Copyright, 1939.)

"FINGER" McGURK, MIKE HENNESSEY'S TRIGGER MAN, LINES UP SUPERMAN AND DISTRICT ATTORNEY LAKE . . . .
IF YOU'VE ANY PRAYERS TO SAY, GET 'EM OVER WITH. THIS IS YOUR FINISH!
YOU MUST BE MAD. AT LEAST A DOZEN REPORTERS SAW YOU ENTER THIS ROOM!
DON'T YOU WORRY ABOUT THAT! I'VE GOT MY PLANS!
WELL . . . WHY DON'T YOU SHOOT?
IT'S THAT GUY-- HE KNOWS I'M GONNA BLOW HIS BRAINS OUT . . . AN YET. . . HE JUST STANDS THERE AN' GRINS!
PARDON ME "FINGER" BUT I JUST CAN'T HELP LAUGHING!
265.
FUNNY. AM I?

Superman—By Jerry Siegel and Joe Shuster *Returning Bullets* (Copyright, 1939.)

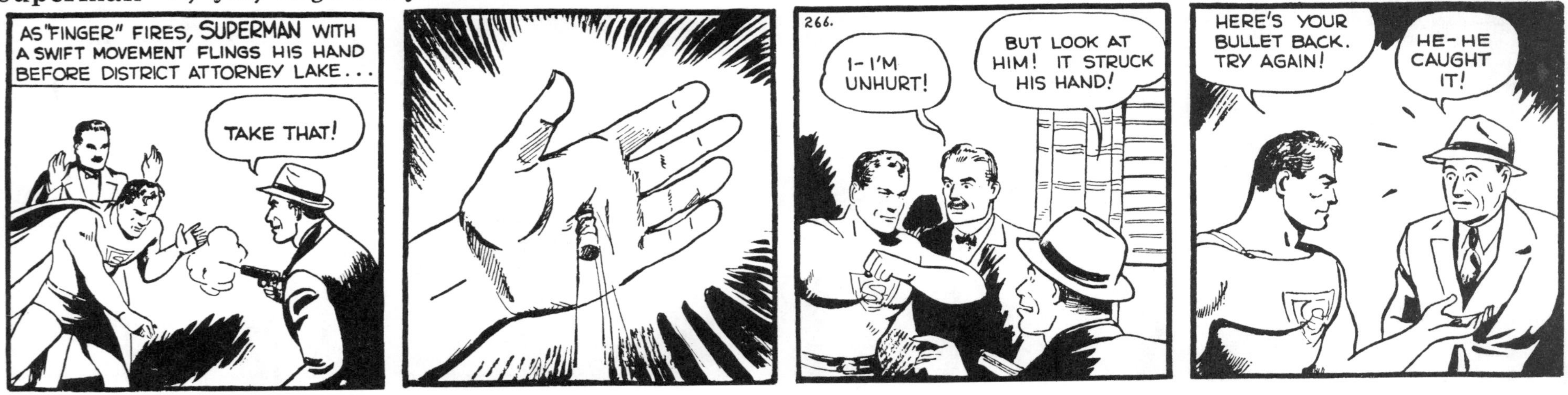
AS "FINGER" FIRES, SUPERMAN WITH A SWIFT MOVEMENT FLINGS HIS HAND BEFORE DISTRICT ATTORNEY LAKE . . .
TAKE THAT!
266.
I-I'M UNHURT!
BUT LOOK AT HIM! IT STRUCK HIS HAND!
HERE'S YOUR BULLET BACK. TRY AGAIN!
HE-HE CAUGHT IT!

Superman—By Jerry Siegel and Joe Shuster *An Invulnerable Target* (Copyright, 1939.)

YA CAUGHT TH' BULLET! BUT THAT'S IMPOSSIBLE! YA COULDN'TA DONE IT!
BUT I DID!
YOU CAN DROP THAT GUN NOW!
K-KEEP AWAY FROM ME! I WARN YA- DON'T TAKE ANOTHER STEP!
AS "FINGER" McGURK EMPTIES HIS WEAPON SUPERMAN DEFLECTS THE HAIL OF BULLETS
267.

Superman—By Jerry Siegel and Joe Shuster *A Swift Return* (Copyright, 1939.)

SUPERMAN LAUGHINGLY CATCHES THE BULLETS FROM "FINGER" McGURK'S GUN . . . . .
. . . TWO, THREE, FOUR . . . !
. . . FIVE, AND SIX! NOW THAT YOUR GUN IS EMPTY, ARE YOU READY TO LISTEN TO REASON?
GOOD LORD!
HE-HE AIN'T HUMAN!
FRANTICALLY, "FINGER" THROWS HIS WEAPON AT SUPERMAN
HOW'S THIS FOR A RETURN?
OW-WW!
268.

Superman—By Jerry Siegel and Joe Shuster *Superman Acts as Valet* (Copyright, 1939.)

THE DISTRICT ATTORNEY WOULD LIKE TO HAVE SOME INFORMATION ABOUT YOUR CON-NECTION WITH "BIG MIKE" HENNESSEY.
LEGGO O' ME! I AIN'T SAYIN' NOTHIN'!
NICE JACKET! MIND IF I BORROW IT?
HEY!
I KINDA GO FOR THAT SHIRT, TOO!
STOP HIM! GET HIM TO STOP!
WHY? I'M ENJOYING THIS!
269.
HM-M-M! THIS NOSE WOULD LOOK PERFECT, MOUNTED ABOVE MY MANTLE PIECE!
STOP! LEGGO! I'LL TELL YA ANYTHING—ANYTHING!
O.K., MR. D.A.! HE'S ALL YOURS!

Superman—By Jerry Siegel and Joe Shuster *The Confession* (Copyright, 1939.)

OUTSIDE THE D.A.'S OFFICE . . .
SHOTS—FROM WITHIN THE OFFICE—!
LET'S BREAK IN!
SOMEONE GET A COP!
270.
NEVER MIND, BOYS—NO ONE'S TO COME IN HERE EXCEPT MY SECRETARY!
GO AHEAD, "FINGER"!
"BIG MIKE" WAS OUR CONTACT WITH THE LAW. FER A PERCENT-AGE OF OUR TAKE, HE'D SQUARE ANYTHING!
WHEN LAKE TURNS TO THANK SUPERMAN
HE'S GONE—MUST HAVE SLIPPED OUT THRU THE OPEN WINDOW!

Superman—By Jerry Siegel and Joe Shuster *A Tough Argument* (Copyright, 1939.)

ANOTHER SCOOP FOR CLARK KENT!
DAILY PLANET
D.A. TRAINS GUNS ON HENNESSEY
"BIG MIKE" LINKED WITH UNDERWORLD
BY CLARK KENT
HERE I AM, STUCK WITH THE LOVELORN COLUMN, WHILE CLARK GETS THE JUICY NEWS ASSIGNMENTS! I'M GOING TO DO SOMETHING ABOUT IT!
EDITOR
271
I'M SICK OF WRITING SENTIMENTAL PAP. I DEMAND A CHANCE AT THE NEWS.
LITTLE GIRL GETTING BORED?
TELL YOU WHAT I'LL DO! BRING ME AN INTERVIEW WITH "BIG MIKE" HENNESSEY, AND I'LL SWITCH YOU TO REPORTING!
"BIG MIKE"! WHY HE EATS REPORTERS ALIVE! DON'T HANDLE THAT YARN!
AFRAID I'LL LAND THE STORY AND STEAL SOME OF YOUR GLORY, EH? JUST FOR THAT, I'LL DO IT!
GO TO IT, LOIS!

Superman—By Jerry Siegel and Joe Shuster *Look Out, Lois.* (Copyright, 1939.)

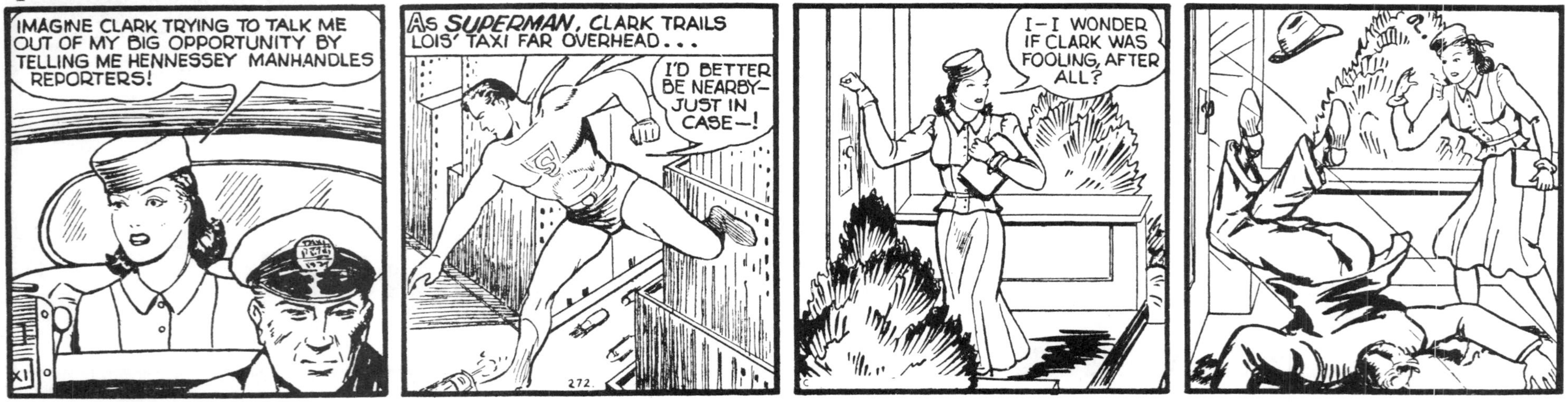
IMAGINE CLARK TRYING TO TALK ME OUT OF MY BIG OPPORTUNITY BY TELLING ME HENNESSEY MANHANDLES REPORTERS!
AS SUPERMAN, CLARK TRAILS LOIS' TAXI FAR OVERHEAD . . .
I'D BETTER BE NEARBY- JUST IN CASE-!
272.
I-I WONDER IF CLARK WAS FOOLING, AFTER ALL?

Superman—By Jerry Siegel and Joe Shuster

Spunky Lois

(Copyright, 1939.)

IT'S BOB STERN—OF THE MORNING PICTORIAL!
DON'T TELL ME YOU'VE COME TO INTERVIEW HENNESSEY?
YES -- WHY NOT?
DON'T DO IT—THE GUY'S CRAZY WITH RAGE! HE'LL SLUG YOU, SURE!
THE DOOR'S OPEN! I'LL PROBABLY GET MY NECK BROKEN—BUT HERE GOES!
273
THE GAL'S CERTAINLY GOT PLENTY OF SPUNK!

Superman—By Jerry Siegel and Joe Shuster

Surprise!

(Copyright, 1939.)

NO ONE IN SIGHT—BUT THERE ARE VOICES AHEAD!
WITHIN A NEARBY ROOM --
YOU'RE A FOOL TO COME HERE TODAY. WHAT IF THE NEWSPAPERS FOUND OUT THAT BUTCH MORGAN, NOTORIOUS GANGSTER, WAS HERE?
SORRY, MIKE! BUT TH' BOYS WANTED TO KNOW WHAT YER GONNA DO ABOUT TH' TRIAL!
SH-H! SOMEONE'S IN THE HALL! GET BEHIND THAT CURTAIN!
GET RID OF 'EM, QUICK!
WELL?
ER -- HELLO!
274

Superman—By Jerry Siegel and Joe Shuster

Hot News!

(Copyright, 1939.)

I'M FROM THE DAILY PLANET. I'D APPRECIATE A SHORT INTERVIEW.
HOW DID YOU GET IN HERE?
I'M TALKING TO NO ONE. GET OUT!
["-SHOES! SOMEONE'S BEHIND THAT CURTAIN!-"]
275.
AW, COME NOW, MR. HENNESSEY— GIVE A GIRL A BREAK!
SCRAM!
["-ANOTHER FEW SECONDS, AND I'LL KNOW WHO IT IS!-"]
BUTCH MORGAN!
WHAT TH'—

Superman—By Jerry Siegel and Joe Shuster

Not So Fast, Lois

(Copyright, 1939.)

THE HONORABLE MIKE HENNESSEY IN CONFERENCE WITH AN UNDERWORLD CHARACTER! WHAT A YARN THAT'LL MAKE!
STOP HER!
WHERE DO YOU THINK YOU'RE GOING?
TO TURN IN THIS STORY. TAKE YOUR HANDS OFF ME!
WHAT'LL WE DO? IF WE LET HER GO SHE'LL SQUAWK!
WE WON'T LET HER GO—AND SHE'LL NEVER SQUAWK!
I GET IT!
SUPERMAN'S X-RAY EYESIGHT APPRISES HIM OF THE SITUATION— AND HE SPRINGS INTO ACTION...!
TIME I TOOK A HAND IN THIS MATTER!
276

Superman—By Jerry Siegel and Joe Shuster *A Better Way* (Copyright, 1939.)

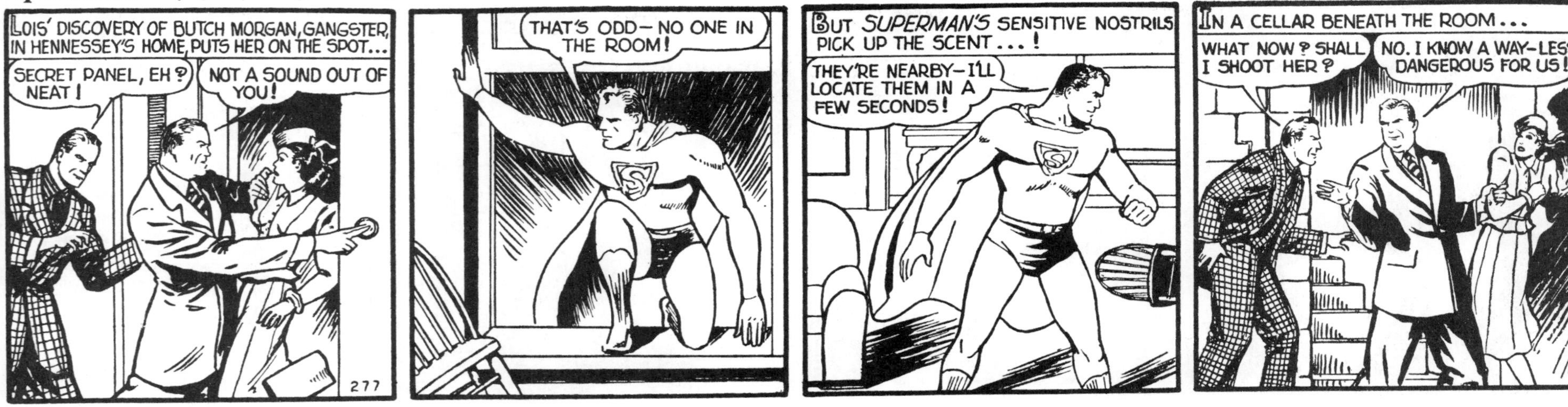
LOIS' DISCOVERY OF BUTCH MORGAN, GANGSTER, IN HENNESSEY'S HOME, PUTS HER ON THE SPOT...
SECRET PANEL, EH? NEAT!
NOT A SOUND OUT OF YOU!
277
THAT'S ODD—NO ONE IN THE ROOM!
BUT SUPERMAN'S SENSITIVE NOSTRILS PICK UP THE SCENT...!
THEY'RE NEARBY—I'LL LOCATE THEM IN A FEW SECONDS!
IN A CELLAR BENEATH THE ROOM...
WHAT NOW? SHALL I SHOOT HER?
NO. I KNOW A WAY—LESS DANGEROUS FOR US!

Superman—By Jerry Siegel and Joe Shuster *Superman Picks Up the Scent* (Copyright, 1939.)

MIKE HENNESSEY TUGS AT A HEAVY SLAB IN THE FLOOR...
WHAT'S THAT?
I CAN REGULATE THE WATER IN THAT PIT. CONVENIENT FOR DISPOSING OF MEDDLERS, EH? HELP ME CHAIN HER.
278.
LET ME OUT. I WON'T TALK!
SHUT YOUR MOUTH!
LOIS' VOICE—BELOW!

Superman—By Jerry Siegel and Joe Shuster *Just in Time* (Copyright, 1939.)

YOU COWARDLY KILLERS!
WHAT TH'-?
HOW'D HE GET IN?
BELIEVE ME, IT IS A PLEASURE TO TAKE YOU TWO ON!
279
BUT MEANWHILE THE WATER LAPS AT LOIS' CHIN—RISES STILL HIGHER...!
SUPERMAN, THANK GOD! HURRY-HURRY!

Superman—By Jerry Siegel and Joe Shuster *Now What?* (Copyright, 1939.)

REACHING DOWN, SUPERMAN EASILY SNAPS THE CHAINS WHICH BIND LOIS...
OUT YOU GO!
CAREFUL—!
Copyright 1939, McClure Newspaper Syndicate
ALL RIGHT, NOW?
YES—BUT THAT WAS A CLOSE CALL.
AS HENNESSEY AND MORGAN REVIVE...
MIND IF I BORROW THIS PENCIL AND PAPER?
WH-WHERE—WHAT—?
280
HEY! LET US DOWN!
WHAT ARE YOU GOING TO DO?
YOU'LL SEE!

Superman—By Jerry Siegel and Joe Shuster *Some of their Own Medicine.* (Copyright, 1939.)

A LITTLE TASTE OF YOUR OWN MEDICINE!
DON'T DO IT— IT'S MURDER!
THAT'S RIGHT— YOU CAN'T DO THIS— IT'S COLD-BLOODED MURDER!
—AN' BESIDES— IT'S AGAINST TH' LAW!
YOU DON'T SAY!
I'LL RELEASE YOU— IF YOU SIGN A CONFESSION OF YOUR CRIMINAL ACTIVITIES.
YOU WOULDN'T LET US DIE! YOU'RE BLUFFING, AND YOU KNOW IT!
I'LL SIGN NOTHIN'!
281
IN THAT CASE I'M OFF—SO LONG, BOYS!

Superman—By Jerry Siegel and Joe Shuster *Signed Confession.* (Copyright, 1939.)

HE'S NOT FOOLIN'— HE'D LET US DIE...!
COME BACK—FOR HEAVEN'S SAKE-WE'LL TELL YOU EVERYTHING!
NOW GENTLEMEN, DICTATE THE DETAILS...!
I'LL GET YOU FOR THIS SOMEHOW!
AND NOW—YOU SIGN TOO—AS A WITNESS...
HEY! WHAT ABOUT US?
HURRY... GET US OUT!
SUPERMAN RELEASES THE SWITCH— SNAPS THE CHAINS THAT BIND THEM, THEN—
MY COLLAR— CAREFUL — YOU'RE CHOKING ME!
SORRY—I HAVEN'T TIME TO BE POLITE!
ULP!
282

Superman—By Jerry Siegel and Joe Shuster

Watch Out, Superman!

SEIZING HENNESSEY AND MORGAN, WHO HAD TRIED TO KILL LOIS, SUPERMAN RETURNS TO THE ROOM ABOVE ....
OUCH! BE CAREFUL!
YOU'RE CRUSHING MY RIBS!
JUST A BUNCH OF SISSIES!
283
THERE—THAT OUGHT TO HOLD YOU!
POLICE HEADQUARTERS? SEND DOWN A SQUAD TO "BIG MIKE" HENNESSEY'S HOME AT ONCE!
WAIT! DON'T GO!
WHY?
I WANT TO TALK TO YOU.
MAKE IT QUICK! "—I'M AFRAID I'M LETTING MYSELF IN FOR SOMETHING!—"

Superman—By Jerry Siegel and Joe Shuster

Lois Is Curious

I'VE ONLY A FEW SECONDS. WHAT IS IT YOU WANT?
YOU'VE NEVER REALLY GIVEN ME A CHANCE TO THANK YOU FOR THE MANY TIMES YOU'VE SAVED MY LIFE.
SAVING YOUR LIFE, CHARMING LADY, IS A PLEASURE FOR WHICH I DESIRE NO THANKS.
AND THERE'S TOO MUCH TO DO FOR ME TO LINGER AFTER MY WORK IS DONE.
BUT WHO ARE YOU? WHERE DO YOU COME FROM? AND WHERE DO YOU GO?
284.

Superman—By Jerry Siegel and Joe Shuster *Solitary Worker* (Copyright, 1939.)

WHERE DO I COME FROM? I DON'T KNOW—BUT I DO KNOW THAT MY SUPER-HUMAN STRENGTH ENABLES ME TO EASE THE COURSE OF JUSTICE.
I HAVE DEDICATED MYSELF TO HELPING THE OPPRESSED—AND SEEING THAT TRUTH AND RIGHT TRIUMPH.
IF ONLY YOU COULD REMAIN AMONG US—AND INSPIRE ORDINARY MORTALS TO FOLLOW YOUR IDEALS!
I FIND I ACHIEVE BEST RESULTS BY—
285.
—PLAYING A LONE HAND!
SUPERMAN! COME BACK!

Superman—By Jerry Siegel and Joe Shuster *A Break for Lois* (Copyright, 1939.)

SINCE LOIS WILL BE REINSTATED ON THE NEWS STAFF IF SHE TURNS IN THIS SCOOP, I'LL PASS UP THE STORY!
286.
SUPERMAN TRANSFORMS HIMSELF INTO CLARK KENT . . .
HERE COME SERGEANT CRANE AND HIS MEN IN RESPONSE TO LOIS' CALL!
HELLO, SERGEANT! ANYTHING IN THE WIND?
YES—COME ALONG!
SOMEONE PHONED HEADQUARTERS, AND—!
LOIS!
ARREST THESE MEN! I HAVE THEIR CONFESSION!

Superman—By Jerry Siegel and Joe Shuster *On the Front Page.* (Copyright, 1939.)

YOU'LL HAVE TO COME ALONG TO THE STATION, MISS.
OKAY, SARGE! I'VE ALREADY PHONED THE STORY TO MY NEWSPAPER—SO MY PAL HERE WON'T BE ABLE TO PIRATE IT!
POLICE HEADQUARTERS...
THIS CONFESSION WILL SMASH THE HENNESSEY POLITICAL MACHINE! CONGRATULATIONS, MISS LANE!
I CAN GO NOW?
YES!
AT LAST! BACK ON THE FRONT PAGE!
I'M GLAD, LOIS—FOR YOUR SAKE!
287.
DAILY PLANET! EXTRA! EXTRA!
THERE'S YOUR STORY! HOW DOES IT FEEL TO BE MAKING HISTORY?
GR-RAND!

Superman—By Jerry Siegel and Joe Shuster *War!* (Copyright, 1939.)

HERE, BOY.
QUITE A THRILL TO READ A FRONT-PAGE STORY WRITTEN BY YOURSELF!
288.
WHAT--?
DAILY PLANET
WAR IN EUROPE
WAR! BUT MY SCOOP,—ON AN INSIDE PAGE!
WOW! THAT'LL MEAN ACTION. LET'S HURRY BACK TO THE OFFICE!

EPISODE TEN
UNNATURAL DISASTERS

Superman—By Jerry Siegel and Joe Shuster

Unconfirmed News

(Copyright, 1939.)

THE DECLARATION OF WAR IN EUROPE HAS THROWN THE DAILY PLANET OFFICE INTO TURMOIL . . .
TELEGRAM FOR EDITOR TAYLOR!
HE'S OUT! I'LL TAKE IT!
289
WHEW!
WESTERN UNION
ELMORE DAM DESTROYED BY MYSTERIOUS EXPLOSION.
AJAX NEWS
CLARK TELEPHONES TO CHECK THE SENSATIONAL STORY . . .
WHAT'S THAT? NOTHING WRONG WITH THE DAM? O.K. THANKS.
["-HM-M!-"]

Superman—By Jerry Siegel and Joe Shuster

It's a Game

(Copyright, 1939.)

ATOP THE DAILY PLANET BUILDING . . .
THERE'S SOMETHING CURIOUS ABOUT THAT DAM STORY! I'M OFF TO INVESTIGATE.
SUPERMAN TEARS ALONG AT BREAKNECK SPEED . . . .
. . . . LEAPING OVER AUTOS IN HIS PATH!
LEAP-FROG!
290

Superman—By Jerry Siegel and Joe Shuster *All's Well, But—* (Copyright, 1939.)

SUPERMAN NEARS HIS DESTINATION.
THE DAM IS INTACT, ALL RIGHT!
THAT TELEGRAM MUST HAVE BEEN A HOAX! THERE'S SOMETHING PHONEY GOING ON HERE.
291.
SUDDENLY, SUPERMAN'S EYES NARROW, AS HIS TELESCOPIC VISION NOTES—? ? ?

Superman—By Jerry Siegel and Joe Shuster *An Unexpected Interruption* (Copyright, 1939.)

WHAT SUPERMAN SAW . . . !
292.
THOSE MEN ARE UP TO SOME MISCHIEF!
ENOUGH DYNAMITE TO BLOW THIS PLACE TO KINGDOM COME!
LET'S GET OUT OF HERE BEFORE WE GO WITH IT!
TNT
AS THE VANDALS TURN TO FLEE, SUPERMAN STREAKS DOWN . . .
LOOK!
WHAT TH-?

Superman—By Jerry Siegel and Joe Shuster

Too Late!

(Copyright, 1939.)

WHAT ARE YOU UP TO?
WHERE DID YOU COME FROM?
HE DROPPED FROM THE SKY!
293.
WILL YOU TELL ME, OR—?
TAKE YOUR HANDS OFF!
WE'VE GOT TO GET AWAY!
I'VE GOT TO STOP THAT FUSE, BEFORE—
IT'S DYNAMITE, YOU FOOL!
IN A FEW SECONDS WE'LL ALL BE BLOWN TO BITS!
TNT

Superman—By Jerry Siegel and Joe Shuster

All Wet

(Copyright, 1939.)

AS SUPERMAN INVESTIGATES, ELMORE DAM EXPLODES . . .
DOWN INTO THE RELEASED WATERS PLUMMETS THE MAN OF TOMORROW . .
294.
. . . SUPERMAN IS SWEPT ALONG BY THE RAGING TORRENT!

THE EXPLOSION OF ELMORE DAM RELEASES A FLOOD IN WHICH SUPERMAN IS SWEPT ALONG . . . !
FAR IN THE DISTANCE, SUPERMAN'S TELESCOPIC VISION SIGHTS . . . .
295.
THE TOWN OF TARRYVILLE--DIRECTLY IN THE PATH OF THE FLOOD!

Superman—By Jerry Siegel and Joe Shuster *A Fantastic Race* (Copyright, 1939.)

SWIMMING SO FAST THAT HIS ARMS APPEAR LIKE PROPELLORS SUPERMAN MAKES HIS WAY FORWARD..
I'VE GOT TO GET TO TARRYVILLE BEFORE THE FLOOD!
. . UNTIL HE BURSTS OUT THRU THE FRONT OF THE GIANT BODY OF WATER RUNNING AMUCK!
PASSED YOU!
THE STRANGEST RACE OF ALL TIME! A MAN--FLEETLY DASHING BEFORE A RAGING FLOOD! WHO WILL WIN—NATURE IN ITS RUGGED FURY OR SUPERMAN?

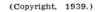

Superman—By Jerry Siegel and Joe Shuster *A Voice From the Mountain* (Copyright, 1939.)

GAINING ON THE FLOOD, SUPERMAN TAKES A TERRIFIC LEAP . . . .
. . . . THAT BRINGS HIM TO A NEARBY MOUNTAIN-TOP !
RIGHT IN THE PATH OF THE FLOOD-AND THE PEOPLE UNAWARE OF THEIR DOOM!
297.
CUPPING HIS HANDS, SUPERMAN SHOUTS A WARNING WHICH CARRIES FOR MILES . . . . !
RUN FOR YOUR LIVES!
THE DAM IS GONE!

Superman—By Jerry Siegel and Joe Shuster *Flight!* (Copyright, 1939.)

THE INHABITANTS OF TARRYVILLE HEAR A STRANGE WARNING FROM THE HEAVENS . . . .
RUN FOR YOUR LIVES!
THE DAM IS GONE!
THAT VOICE-FROM NOWHERE!
IT'S DOOMSDAY!
HURRIEDLY, THE FAMILIES PACK WHATEVER POSSESSIONS THEY CAN...
DRUGS
... AND START A HASTY EXODUS !
THEY CAN'T ESCAPE IN TIME—UNLESS....

Superman—By Jerry Siegel and Joe Shuster

What Can Superman Do?

(Copyright, 1939.)

SUPERMAN STREAKS DOWN....
....AND DROPS DIRECTLY IN THE PATH OF THE MOUNTAINOUS WALL OF WATER!
299
I'LL LICK YOU AND SAVE TARRYVILLE!

Superman—By Jerry Siegel and Joe Shuster

He Stems the Flood

(Copyright, 1939.)

WITH THE SPEED OF LIGHT, SUPERMAN TEARS AT THE LAND SCATTERING SOIL LIKE RAIN....
IN A FEW MINUTES HE HAS DUG A PIT MORE THAN A MILE LONG!
NOT MUCH TIME TO ACT!
300
AS THE TONS OF WATER ROAR DOWN INTO THE GIANT HOLE....
GOTTA SCRAM!

SUPERMAN No Thanks Necessary By Jerry Siegel and Joe Shuster

AS THE FLOOD FAILS TO SWEEP DOWN UPON THEM, THE FLEEING CITIZENS OF TARRYVILLE HALT IN ASTONISHMENT...
WHAT'S HAPPENED?
LOOK!
SORRY I HAD TO CHANGE THE SCENERY IN THIS VALLEY-- BUT IT SAVED THEIR LIVES!
301.
AS THEIR AMAZING RESCUER LEAPS OFF, A TREMENDOUS CHEER OF GRATITUDE RISES FROM THE ASTONISHED ONLOOKERS . . .!
GLORY BE!
HE—HE'S NOT HUMAN!
DON'T CARE WHAT HE IS— HE'S SAVED OUR LIVES!
MUCH OBLIGED!
DON'T MENTION IT!

Superman—By Jerry Siegel and Joe Shuster *Superman's Guess Confirmed.*

THERE'S SOMETHING MIGHTY PECULIAR ABOUT THE AJAX NEWS AGENCY ANNOUNCING THE DESTRUCTION OF THE DAM BEFORE IT OCCURRED. I THINK I'LL GIVE THAT OUTFIT THE ONCE-OVER!
302.
SUPERMAN'S FIGURE COMETS DOWNWARD! AN OUTTHRUST HAND CATCHES THE WINDOW LEDGE OF THE NEWS AGENCY'S OFFICE . . .
IN THE ROOM . . .
FOOL! YOU SENT OUT THAT NEWS DISPATCH HALF AN HOUR TOO EARLY!
IT WAS AN UNFORTUNATE MISTAKE! I NEVER INTENDED...
OUR SUPERIORS HAVE WAYS OF "DISCOURAGING" MISTAKES, GIGGI!
MY GUESS WAS RIGHT! THESE MEN ARE RESPONSIBLE FOR THE DISASTER. WELL, HERE'S WHERE THEY GET A TASTE OF DISASTER!

Superman—By Jerry Siegel and Joe Shuster

Fifteen Minutes To Go!

SUPERMAN, ABOUT TO CONFRONT THE PLOTTERS, PAUSES WHEN HE OVERHEARS...
("-WAIT! -")
YOU MAY HAVE FUMBLED THAT DISPATCH, MY MUDDLE-HEADED GIGGI, BUT THERE WILL BE NO SUCH ERROR IN CONNECTION WITH THE RESERVOIR!
NO ONE WILL KNOW THAT THE REMSON RESERVOIR HAS BEEN POLLUTED UNTIL THE BACTERIA-POISONED WATER FLOWS INTO THE CITY-IN ABOUT FIFTEEN MINUTES!
I'LL ATTEND TO THEM LATER!
MY IMMEDIATE CONCERN IS TO PREVENT THE POISONED WATER FROM BEING CHANNELLED INTO THE CITY!
303.

Superman—By Jerry Siegel and Joe Shuster

Stubborn Opposition

NOT A SECOND TO LOSE! I'VE GOT TO WARN THE --
RAISE YOUR HANDS-OR I'LL BLOW YOU TO BLAZES!
AND WHO ARE YOU?
ME? I'M THE MAN IN CHARGE HERE, AND IF YOU MAKE A FALSE MOVE, MISTER, I'LL BLOW YOUR THIEVIN' HEAD OFF!
YOU'RE JUST THE MAN I WANT TO SEE. THE WATER MUSN'T BE RELEASED- IT'S LOADED WITH DEADLY BACTERIA!
HEY, FELLER, WHAT'S YOUR GAME? I'M NOT AS GULLIBLE AS YOU THINK!
IT'S TIME FOR THE WATER TO BE RELEASED! DON'T TRY ANYTHING!
YOU FOOL! THOUSANDS OF LIVES MAY BE THE PRICE OF YOUR STUPIDITY!

Superman—By Jerry Siegel and Joe Shuster

Look Out, Blackie!

(Copyright, 1940.)

LET GO! I'VE GOT TO DO MY JOB – I'VE ORDERS!
NO, YOU DON'T! SINCE YOU WON'T BELIEVE THE WATER IS POISONED, I'LL HAVE TO STOP YOU FORCIBLY!
SIC 'IM BLACKIE!
COMPANY, EH?
HI 'YA, POOCH!
DON'T MAKE FRIENDS WITH HIM, BLACKIE! ATTACK HIM!
HE'S LAPPING UP SOME OF THE WATER TRICKLING FROM THE WHEEL!
NO, BLACKIE! NO!
305.

Superman—By Jerry Siegel and Joe Shuster

A Canine Martyr

(Copyright, 1940.)

TOO LATE! HE'S DRUNK SOME OF THE WATER!
BLACKIE!
306.
HE'S DEAD! THE BEST PAL A MAN EVER HAD!
I'M SORRY. BUT I TRIED TO WARN YOU!
YOU SPOKE THE TRUTH! BUT HOW DID YOU KNOW?
SORRY I CAN'T ENLIGHTEN YOU ON THAT!
YOU'VE DIED, BLACKIE – BUT NOT IN VAIN! THE THOUSANDS WHO WERE SAVED BECAUSE OF YOU WILL ALWAYS BLESS YOUR NAME!